Tales of a Lincolnshire Parson

by
Canon John Swaby

Stories • Memories • History • Verse

Published by
Louth **N**aturalists', **A**ntiquarian and **L**iterary **S**ociety
The Museum, 4 Broadbank, Louth LN11 0EQ
(Tel : 01507 601211)
2004

**For my daughter Sara
and my grandchildren Fiona & Robert**

Printed in Great Britain by Allinson Print & Supplies
Queen Street, Louth, Lincolnshire LN11 9BN. Telephone: 01507 606661

Contents

Front Cover: **Centre:** *Louth St James.* Clockwise:
Scunthorpe St John, Mablethorpe St Mary
Barton St Mary and Uffington St Michael

St James's Church, Louth
(Mary Swaby)

Preface

This book is almost entirely about Lincolnshire for my roots are deep in the county. I was born in the Marsh at Withern in 1911. Both my parents were born in the county, as were my ancestors on both sides as far back as I can trace them, which is a little over 200 years. On my paternal side it must go back much farther. After all, our surname derives from a Wolds village.

I hope the first person singular will not appear too much as this is not an autobiography and a nonagenarian's anecdotage can be boring. In a few places I have tried to reproduce the expressive mid-Lincolnshire dialect. One of its features is that if two vowels come together they are sounded as two. Thus road becomes ru-ad. And when a long 'a' occurs it is doubled. Thus mate becomes may-at. There are many subtleties and variations, sounding make as mek for example. I'm no expert but I know what I used to hear.

Following the Tales and Stories are chapters adapted from articles which I contributed to *Lincolnshire Past & Present*: 'WWI at Wainfleet' in Spring of 2000, 'Louth Imps' in Winter 2000/01, 'Touches of Tennyson' in Autumn 1999 and 'Memories of Mablethorpe' in Autumn 2002. The poem appended to Scunthorpe St John's is one which I wrote down as soon as I awoke from the dream. The verses on '31st January 1953' appeared in *The Lincolnshire Poacher* Winter 2000.

'Thunder over the Wold' began as something my wife and I sent in place of a Christmas card in 1987, and later appeared in the *Lincolnshire Historical and Archeological Society Newsletter*. Use is made of the few details we know about one man in the hope that with a little imagination Henry Robling may be brought to life. 'A Heave of Churchyards' appeared in the *Lincoln Diocesan Magazine* in 1976, and 'Three Friends' is abridged from an article in the same magazine 1974/75. 'Preacher & Sexton' is an attempt to make something interesting out of a list of funeral expenses.

The aim in the verses is to include one for each part of Lincolnshire with which I have been associated. 'Old St Peter's' had appeared in my *Random Rhymes* (1989) and in *The Lincolnshire Poacher* Summer 2002. Others have come from *Memories of a Lincolnshire Parson* (2001) which had a private circulation, and 'The Cricket Match' and 'Janna' are included for light relief. 'Swaledale' appears because it was there I started writing verse, and 'Start of the Third Millennium' was used by the Archbishop of Canterbury on his Christmas card. To illustrate some of the verses and elsewhere, I have included little drawings done by my late wife Mary a few years ago.

I am greatful to David Robinson for his help in editing and designing this book, and to Louth 'Ants and Nats' for publishing it to mark the 70th anniversary of my ordination, which took place in St James's Church, Louth.

The author at Uffington 1975

Chapter 1

Tales Told To Me

WAINFLEET St Mary's parish was once described as containing nearly six thousand acres of land and over seven thousand of water. The latter must have been in the undrained East Fen. The church nestled under the old fen bank. From there to the sea bank it was a journey of five and more miles. Once the Vicar and I cycled to visit a dying man who lived under that bank in a cottage exposed to biting winds, devoid of hedges and sparse in trees. When he died he was buried in the distant churchyard, and on the following Sunday evening three of the family came to church. As I walked home with a farm worker the family passed us. A more vigorous son drove a motor-cycle. In the sidecar was the widow and on the pillion seat was one I will call Billy. My companion told me the following tale about Billy.

In the First World War he was called up for the forces and sent to France. He had never been as much as ten miles away from his lonely home before and men in a mass bewildered him. Being rather simple he could not learn the drill. After much lurid language the sergeant put him on a defaulter's parade. "I'll take the parade," the captain said. "I'll teach the ruddy lot." He then mounted a horse and chased men around the square. At last all but one had dropped completely exhausted to the ground. Billy, however, remained erect. Horses had no terror for him and following the plough from dawn to dusk he had acquired one pace. That he could keep up almost endlessly. It was the captain who retired beaten. They put Billy in the cookhouse, but he was useless there. They finally sent him home under escort. He was discharged. I wonder if he ever dreamed of seeing the captain behind a plough or the sergeant dealing with a crazy Lincolnshire curly coat. Perhaps he had not enough imagination for that.

* * * * *

I was a curate in Louth for seven happy years. There I was told about eccentric Miss Allenby and a former curate. She took a liking to him and went to his lodgings with bottles of port. The poor man told his landlady to say that he was out. "Then I shall come in and wait," said Miss Allenby. The unhappy man got under the table where fortunately the cloth was very large. Then the church bell began to ring out loudly for Evensong and he was on duty. All he could do was come out and run. Miss Allenby regularly attended weekday Evensong. A plumber once told me that one evening she was passing the foot of his ladder when the bell stopped. Her reaction was to beat her flank with a riding crop and exclaim, "Damn it, Lu Lu, you're late".

I was also told about the mill which crowned the hill on the Horncastle Road. A number of Jehovah's Witnesses came from America to warn their relatives in Louth that the end of the world would come on a certain day. When that day arrived the little party gathered at that high point just after dawn. Word got around and people came to stare. At last, as darkness fell, the party retired. And throughout that day at least a few local people had met their unseen Lord in prayer and sacrament.

It was in Louth also that I heard a story told about a neighbouring cleric who was generous with his money and far from sparing in the length of his discourse. Having heard him preach once I could appreciate the story. He was taking the chair at a meeting and took so long over his introductory remarks that when the guest speaker's turn came he could only say, "The chairman has told you all about the subject and I have a train to catch. I bid you good day".

I was once at a Clergy Chapter meeting when a wonderful howler was made by a very earnest priest who had the unhappy knack of expressing himself badly. He lamented the state of the finances of his village church school. "Cannot Major Ingoldby help?" What the parson then meant to say was "He has the expenses of keeping a son at the Dartmouth Naval Training College," but what he actually said was, "He's got a son at Dartmoor".

* * * * *

I was vicar of Scunthorpe from December 1940 to April 1953. My predecessor was called Steele. Rust was at Frodingham and Greeson at Crosby. So there had been the inevitable riddle and answer: What do you do when there's rust on steel? Put Greeson.

Soon after I went to Scunthorpe an elderly man told me about Billy Hilbert who, when the church was built in 1891, lived in a cottage where later the Ashdown Memorial Hall stood. Wearing a smock and a slouch hat, Billy would stand at his door watching the workmen until he discovered that they were carving his head on the side of the west window of the north aisle. He then refused to come out until the men went off for lunch. The men then put a screen over the window and left a man behind, hoping that through a slit he might memorise Billy's face. But the sly old man would count the workmen as they arrived and as they left. The man who told me the story was then a boy. He was smuggled up behind the screen in the course of the morning and came down at lunchtime wearing a workman's overalls. That made the count correct so Billy came out again to gaze. It is said that when Billy saw the finished carving he tried to smash it. But perhaps he was half proud.

Another Scunthorpe story relates to a Flixborough man. He would walk into Scunthorpe on a Saturday night. Returning along Normanby Road he heard footsteps behind him. He quickened his pace and so did the steps. He ran and they came on faster. At last, breathless he turned round and shouted, "Satan, I defy you. You cannot hurt me. I sing in Flixborough Church Choir twice every Sunday". Then from the darkness came the bray of an escaped donkey.

*   *   *   *   *

From 1953 to late 1960 I was rector of Mablethorpe St Mary with Stain, Rector of Theddlethorpe St Helen with Mablethorpe St Peter and Vicar of Theddlethorpe All Saints. As St Peter's had been under the sea for five hundred years, *The Church Times* suggested that a bathing costume would be appropriate for an induction ceremony. I shall refer to pluralities again.

Among our friends were Miss Whitelaw, daughter of the first resident rector for three hundred years, and Mrs Whitehead, daughter of Dr Smyth who was reputed to be able to lecture on any subject even if he knew little about it. He rode a tricycle around his parishes. One night he rode into a deep ditch and called out for help. A passing labourer shouted out, "Who's there?" Smyth replied, "The Vicar of Sutton on Sea, Hannah cum Markby and Hagnaby," whereupon the labourer said, "If there are so many of you, you can help each other out".

Mrs Whitehead could tell a lively tale, but I cannot vouch for this one relating to Lincolnshire. The Rural Dean had invited the clergy to a meal and a meeting, and as one shy man lived rather a long way away he was asked to stay the night. Next morning at breakfast the hostess nervously said, "Mr X, I hope you were all right. That was the only room to spare, and it is said to be haunted." To her relief he said he had been comfortable. Then he added, "Someone came in , but I was busy with some accounts I looked up and said, 'We are rather in debt. Can I put you down for a donation?' At that he quickly disappeared."

A Theddlethorpe man told me how going into Mablethorpe one day he encountered a native and the following conversation ensued. "How are things?". The native answered, "Not well, but maybe the good Lord will send us a wreck". In that part they liked a wreck, but were not wreckers, and there are true stories of men riding horses out into the storm when a lifeboat could not be launched. Some ship had been stranded on the shallow shore and was breaking up beneath battering waves. They rode back with the crews. There was also much smuggling, but I have told tales of that in *The Marshmen*, which has long been out of print.

In Theddlethorpe they told of how All Saints' Hall was haunted by the ghost of the drunkard Will Duckering. His wife hid the key to the beer cellar, but one day both key and he were missing. She found the door open and there was Will, on his back with his open mouth below the turned on tap of the beer barrel, dead. None of my friends the Shelbourns had seen his ghost.

Once Theddlethorpe had had its own doctor. One night he was awakened by a girl calling outside the house. He stuck his head out of the window and asked what the trouble was. A well known voice said, "Please sir, it's me mum. She can neither sit nor lig". "Then tell the old devil she can fly till the morning."

I called to see an old lady living in that house. Once she had lived in Withern where I was born. She told me the story of the Withern farmer who went as usual each week to Alford Market and, as usual, he drank too much. His friends did not worry as they put him in his trap; the horse knew the way home. He got home to find his wife had gone to bed. In the kitchen before the fire was a large bowl of dough which had been left overnight to rise. He mistook this for his favourite arm chair, sank into it and could not get out. In answer to his shouts his wife came downstairs, only to inform him that he could stay there until morning. Thinking the old lady might have more stories, I called again next day. She could not even remember the one she had told me.

On our mantelpiece is a cream jug given to us by Ted Badley when we married. His mother used to bring it out when the vicar came to tea. It had belonged to Lot Ward, a Methodist local preacher. The story of Lot and the miller is told in *The Marshmen* but I will tell it again as I did there.

Waard was a great preacher an 'e could praay till 'e was a lather o' sweat. Waard was 'avin a mishun in this 'ere plaace. Hevangelisin' is wot they calls it. Soa 'e goas to the mill 'ouse, an 'e axes if the miller would cum to 'ear 'im in the chappil. "Noa," sez the miller. "Yer can saave yersen wi'out werritin' me." "If ya weant 'ear me preach, the I'll praay for yer," sez owd Lot. "I doant want nowt", sez the miller, an' 'e starts to cloase the door. But theare weren't no stoppin' Lot. He plumps down on 'is kneas. "Lawd", e sez, "Thou knawest wot we are an' we cum afoare Thee beggin' for Thy mercy, an' we praay Thee that Thou wouldest sent Thy wind to ton the saals of our brother's mill soa 'e can grind the weat an' prase Thy Naame".

Next daay the miller goas lookin' for Lot and wen 'e catched 'im he sez, "Yer praayed for wind yisterdaay". "Aye," sez Lot, "an' praase the Lawd it cumed." "Dang yer, yer nivver cud let well aloane. Yer praayed at mi door, but yer nivver sed nowt about praayin' in the chappil. Yer did an' thear were soa much wind in the night it brokk the saals."

I also heard in Theddlethorpe of two tipsy men going home one night when they came to a plank bridge over a broad stream. They knew the one way to get across was to run over before there was time to think. One man got across, but the other lost his nerve halfway, swayed and fell into the slime. As he emerged the first man sang part of a well-known hymn:

> 'Part of the host has crossed the flood,
> And part is crossing now'.

Ditches in the Marsh could be very dangerous. Not long before he was nominated Bishop of Durham, Bishop Harland of Lincoln had planned to preach in Mablethorpe. When the nomination was made, I suggested he might like to be excused. He still came. The church was reached by a bridge over a deep drain. As we crossed it the Bishop paused and said, "I always thought I should end my days in one of these".

I have written about Ted Badley in *Random Rhymes*, but I cannot refrain from repeating one of his tales. He died a bachelor, but liked to tell how he had once asked a girl to marry him. She had replied, "I don't want to be badly all my life".

It was perhaps while I was still in the Marsh that I heard the story of the woman sexton at Welton le Wold, which was united with Louth. She kept the church in such a good condition that a visitor once asked her why some people felt it was necessary to pay for the upkeep of the graves of relatives. She answered, "Them as pays gets the shears and them as doesn't gets the 'ook."

It was while I was still in the Marsh that Canon Morris, a retired and much loved rector of Skegness, told me of his experience when taking a mission at one of the three Saltfleetbys. The evening service was over the verger was putting out the oil lamps when a man who had stayed behind drew a knife, approached Morris and said, "Mr Morris, you are too good for this world. I will help you to the next." Although Morris was a pacifist he promptly felled the man with a single blow. The next day the would-be assassin was sent to a mental hospital.

*   *   *   *   *

I was vicar of Barton on Humber from 1960 to 1971. I then became rector of the Uffington Group, eighty miles away but still in the diocese of Lincoln. A General Bertie who lived there succeeded to the Bertie estates and to the earldom of Lindsey when he was quite old. He married the rector's sister and had three children quickly. Charlotte, the eldest, was only six when he died. She was to become an able and gifted woman. One had only to read her diaries to know that. The second child, George Augustus Frederick, became the tenth earl in 1909. His mother then married a cousin called Peter Pegus, an unstable clergyman. He made the children's life a misery. The following story about the earl and Pegus was told to us by the delightful Robin Lowe, one of whose ancestors made the lovely churchyard gates.

In order to get control of the estate, Pegus tried to have George Augustus declared insane. A doctor was called in. He questioned the mentally retarded earl. "How many legs has a sheep?" The earl replied, "Two." That, thought the doctor, settles the matter. It did not when the earl added, "Two legs and two shoulders." Before she died the Dowager Countess expressed the wish that Pegus should have the rectory of Uffington at the next vacancy. Her wishes were ignored and Pegus was given an annuity on condition that he kept away from Uffington.

*   *   *   *   *

12

So far I have limited my stories to places where I was curate or incumbent. But I now mention something that happened in the Marsh when I was rural dean there. The rectory for the united benefice of All Saints and St Peter's, Saltfleetby was most unsuitable. The awful kitchen on the east side might do for servants but not for a cookless rector's wife. The western part had high and sunny rooms. Many turned the vacant benefice down. When a possible candidate asked me if I would bring my wife here I had to say, "No". There were about six steps down from the newer part to the bathroom in the old. We were able to persuade the diocese that large scale alterations were needed and a man accepted the benefice because his wife had relatives in the area. Wisely he would not move in until the alterations were completed. Months dragged by. Then one of the churchwardens, a man from Sheffield, decided to stir things up. He summoned a church meeting to which I was invited. After he had spoken for a long time he asked me to explain the legal position. When I had finished a farmer's wife expressed her opinion in a blunt way and in typical Lincolnshire dialect: "If what the rural dean tells us is true, why are we wasting our time?" And straightaway the ladies began to plan the meal to be held after the induction, whenever that might be.

I have also been told tales about other parts of the county. A man who had been a curate in Grimsby related how he had been accustomed to knocking and then walking into a particular house in the parish. One night he thought he was doing so, but when inside realised that he was in the wrong terrace house. He retreated quickly but the people inside heard him and pursued the intruder. He managed to run round a corner, and then turned round. When the pursuers arrived and asked him if they had seen anyone, he calmly said 'no' and retraced his steps.

A Grimsby incumbent who had been a curate in Lincoln told how he looked up to an uncurtained window and saw an old man trying to cook his supper in a pan over a candle. He made enquiries and heard the following tale. It was in the days when the church of St Peter at Arches stood near the bridge over the Witham. It was the corporation church and the most important church downhill. The curate was a brilliant preacher and if the people knew he was going to preach the congregation was always greater, The incumbent was away for a long time. Then one Sunday night the curate excelled himself. He preached the incumbent's obituary sermon. But the incumbent was not dead. He was back there in church. That night the curate turned up in his nightshirt at the Bishop's Palace. His unconscious wishes had caused a breakdown. He was the old man with the pan and candle.

Mr Cholmoley (pronounced Chumley), the old parson of Keddington by Louth, told me the following story. He had seen hanging in the porch of a Norfolk church a very long surplice with cuts in the hem. It was one of several parishes held by the arch-deacon. When he arrived to take a service he had no time to robe within or to take off his spurs. The cuts were caused by spurs as he walked up the church reciting the opening sentences. I still have Mr Cholmoley's violet stole. He was related to the family mentioned in the next chapter. He may have told me about 'The King of the Marsh'.

The head of Billy Hibbert carved on St John's Church, Scunthorpe

Chapter 2

Stories I Have Read

ROBERT Cholmoley became rector of Wainfleet All Saints in 1817 and a little later took charge of St Mary's also. One of his daughters married Marshall Heanley, a Croft farmer. Because of his great strength he was known as 'The King of the Marsh', and the story is told of how he quietened two noisy men by picking one up in each arm and banging their heads together. Their son Robert tells how he and his mother visited someone in Croft suffering from ague. They had brought quinine, but the family knew better. Someone picked up a hammer and struck the bed end, reciting,

> Fayther, Son and 'oly Ghoast,
> Nail the devil to this poast,
> Thrice I strike wi' 'oly crook,
> One for God and one for Wod and one for Lok.

Heanley was very interested in traces of the Vikings and suggested that here was a mixture of Christianity and paganism. The holy crook was also the hammer of Thor, Wod was the Norse God Wodin, and Lok was Loki, the Norse spirit of evil.

In 1880, Robert Heanley became rector of Wainfleet All Saints. He tells how a wheelwright on the Bank (possibly Ebenezer Chambers) called him to look at a sick pig. Heanley suggested whiskey and was told, "Nay, thou knawest better nor that. I du knaw that she hev been overluked and thou knaws the party that ev dun it. If I nobbut cud draw blud of shea it ud be all reight, but then shea hev the law on me and they magistraates up in Spilsby be that iggorant they ud mak me paay; so I thott as maybe you ud saay a few wods ower the sow and set her free." When the rector declined the wheelwright asked for a piece of the wicken (rowan or mountain ash) that grew near the gate of Northolme Hall where the rector lived. The rector again declined, but thought that the man must have helped himself, for the next time he went that way there was a sprig of wicken over the sty. Wicken was regarded as affording protection against witchcraft and, if there was an outbreak of swine fever, it was found over every pigsty in the district.

I no longer have a copy of *Folklore concerning Lincolnshire* by Mrs Gutch and Mabel Peacock, but am fairly sure that it was there that I read a story about Messingham. A visitor to that place noticed the absence of church bells and gave three men money to rectify matters. Some time later he returned and heard the sounds Ting-Tong-Pluff coming from the church tower. He had apparently given the money to a blacksmith, a carpenter and a leather worker, and each had constructed a bell out of material in which he was accustomed to work.

J. A. Penny, vicar of Stixwould and Wispington, published *More Folklore Round Horncastle* in 1922. The first and best story is entitled 'A Painful Parting'. He heard it from an old man about thirty years earlier. An ambitious young cleric, who had more zeal than gumption, had managed to upset most of the parishioners so when he went round the parish to say that the Bishop had offered him another living, there were few expressions of regret. Some said 'It will be nice for you to have a change' or 'How kind of the Bishop'. None said anything to satisfy his conceit.

He had never been on good terms with 'the straight Un', so he left her visit to the end. She surprised him by bursting into tears. He promised to come back to see her, but she was inconsolable. Then he asked why she was so upset and she replied, "There was So-and-So who was good to nobody. So-and-So got drunk, So-and-So shut himself up with his books until he was crazed. We always get someone worse. When you came I said 'They do pick 'em for this place'. If you are going the Owd Lad himself must be coming."

George Hall, sometimes rector of Ruckland, had published *The Gypsy's Parson* in 1915. In his diary for that year, Bishop Edward Lee Hicks described Hall as a nice looking fellow, rather grey, nicely spoken and a keen scholar in gypsy lore. Hall dedicated his book to his wife, who was by that time paralysed. She had been his companion on many a 'gypsy jaunt.'

Hall was walking down a town street on his way to an Archdeacon's Visitation when he saw an elderly gypsy woman. He greeted her in Romany. She refused an offer of tobacco, but accompanied Hall into a nearby coffee house. The conversation in Romany mystified the prim looking manageress whose curiosity kept her hovering around. At last the gypsy gave Hall a sly look and said in English,

"Never mind him, missis, he's an Irishman, and can't a boy and his mother talk a word or two in their own language?". As she left the old gypsy said, "The Lord love you my son, and may you have a large hedgehog for your breakfast."

One story relates to Stow, now in the parish of Threekingham. In the reign of Henry III Sempringham Priory was granted the right to have a three-day fair there on the eve of St John the Baptist's Day. The church had long gone and Hall says the only building on Stow Green, the site of the fair, was a dilapidated lock up. The affair was an occasion of drunkenness and disorder.

Wandering in and out of the motley throng, Hall heard there was to be a fight. When a quarrel arose between two gypsy families, the matter was usually settled there. Hall climbed on a trestle table outside a booth to get a good view. The champions of two Gray families were stripped to the waist. When blood was drawn the crowd grew very excited and the police hurried up, but decided not to intervene. "Let 'em have it out", yelled the crowd. As a heavy blow ended the fight, the table on which Hall and others stood collapsed and various jugs and glasses from the booth were broken. As he recalled the fight, Hall remembered an old song:

> 'Whack it in the grinders, thump it on the jaw,
> Smack it on the tater-trap a dozen times or more,
> Slap in on the snuff box, make the claret fly,
> Thump it on the jaw again, never say die.'

Once a gypsy cab driver took Hall to an afternoon service in a village church. Neither had been there before, but the driver was confident he knew the way. A few minutes before three o'clock Hall was set down outside an old stone church. He found the congregation already assembled, and went under the tower to ask the verger where the vestry was. The verger explained that there was no vestry, and that their parson robed at home, and then came in through a little door. He led Hall to a chantry chapel. After Hall had robed, and the bell had ceased, he went towards the prayer desk. At that moment a fully robed old parson came in through the chancel door. "Sir, I am afraid there has been a mistake", stammered Hall. The old man shook his head sadly. "I am very deaf. I cannot hear a word." He then knelt down at the desk. The choir giggled and the congregation tittered. It was left to the lady organist to tell Hall that he had come to the wrong church.

Tales of a Lincolnshire Antiquary was written by Canon George Gilbert Walker who died in 1933, but edited by W.A. Cragg and printed in

Sleaford in 1949. Walker had been incumbent of four different Lincolnshire parishes and described himself as a Lincolnshire man through and through. He left Huttoft in 1893. In his successor's time a service had been arranged and for it the choir was to proceed from the vicarage to the church. Some people waited outside the church porch to see the unusual sight. A distant sound was heard and a lady from another parish said, "I think I hear the choir". A farmer replied, "Oh, no, ma'am, that's my turkeys a gawblin' ". It was in fact the choir.

On a warm Whitsunday in 1890 one of the old school, whom Walker calls the Reverend Joseph, was robed in the vestry. He was waiting for a visitor who would help with the service. He wore a very long surplice buttoned at the neck. Beneath he wore a long overcoat. "Rector", asked the churchwarden, "why are you wearing a winter overcoat on a warm day?". The rector answered, "Stranger come to preach don't you know, thought I'd put on something that looked like a cassock".

As this man and his wife grew old she urged him to extend the family vault in the churchyard. It had been built to hold four and it already contained the bodies of Joseph's father, his wife and unmarried daughter. "No ma'am," said Joseph. "So long as we are man and wife we'll go on as we are, but then I'm going in that vault and you'll be in a plain grave outside with no bricks." She was regarded as socially inferior. Perhaps one does not wonder why Methodism attracted the middle and lower classes.

I have mentioned stories from these books because they are only to be found, if one is lucky, in a second-hand book shop. The short piece which appeared in *The Church Times* of something that happened a hundred years earlier is perhaps the last place where one would expect to find information about the Rev Joseph Charles Edwards who became rector of Ingoldmells in 1864 with a salary of £160 p.a. He was a man who had great ideas and few resources to carry them out.

G.H.J. Dutton's *Skegness and District* says that Edwards was a popular preacher and in spite of his eccentricity many came in their own carriages to hear him. In January 1967 *The Church Times* related how a hundred years earlier Edwards had appeared before the Bankruptcy Court for examination and discharge. His debts amounted to as much as £2,331 but his assets to only £70. He said that he had married in 1858 but separated from his wife in the same year. He had been in difficulty for some time. He admitted in writing to Mr Duckworth a creditor, "I have expended £200 in church schools and rectory and do not deceive yourself that any machinations of devil, clerics or lawyers will harass me. I soar above such things and treat with supreme contempt the miserable efforts of buffoons to vex my indomitable spirit". *The Church Times* said that this produced laughter and added, "Mr Edwards is of course an anti-ritualist". It does not record that when questioned in court as to why he owed a draper £60 when there were no ladies in his establishment he replied, "I tell you that it is a great condescension for me to be questioned by you". Kelly's Directory for 1876 says that the church had been much restored in 1866.

The Church Times seems to gloat over Edwards' downfall, for in the previous December it had waxed indignant over the scene in a Manchester Nonconformist chapel when "Mr Edwards, wearing a black gown, ascended the pulpit". In the course of the sermon Edwards had said, "It was earnest zeal after God that created Christ's presence; it was not the lofty music, the splendid cathedral, the garments of the priest or the sacrament". He concluded by saying that during the sermon he never thought he was preaching in a place different from his own church. "Mankind must enter heaven not as Episcopalians or Congregationalist, but as believers in Christ". He did not know that there was anything in the New Testament about bishops, priests and deacons; if there was it was episcopacy that was a very moderate one.

In *Parson's Pleasure*, Bishop W.S. Swayne referred to Edwards. "He was often in prison but bore his misfortune with a gentle equanimity, and would send his nightshirt to gaol so that it might be properly aired before his arrival." How does one describe Edwards? The words 'gentle equanimity' do not seem adequate and he was more than eccentric. The word 'megalomaniac' seems too strong. Perhaps one can say that here was a gifted man who somehow thought that the usual habits of financial prudence and courtesy did not apply to him. Kelly's Directory for 1876 records that Edwards was still rector, but there was a curate in charge.

I shall end this chapter with a tale of my own. I called on a lady in a large house. She came from a wealthy industrial family and two volumes had been written about the history of her husband's family. She never turned a cat away and when at last her relatives intervened over twenty were destroyed. She was very deaf and ringing the front door bell produced no response. So a raw young curate nervously walked up the small flight of stairs that led to the sitting room. Through the open door he saw her at an open window, fondling a cat. In order not to startle her, I bounced up and down on the floorboards until she felt the vibrations. Then sat down. "Would you like a piece of cake?". It seemed polite to accept the offer. Unfortunately the cat went to the cupboard and walked all over the cake. It was not easy to explain on a slate that it would be much nicer to take the slice of cake home and have it with one's tea. The birds did well from the visit. When next seen the old lady was sitting up in bed looking neat and tidy. There were only two cats.

Rev George Hall
The Gypsy's Parson

Chapter 3

Memories of World War 1 in Wainfleet

I WAS born in 1911, so these memories come from early childhood. During the Great War the Coronation Hall was used as a military convalescent hospital with Mrs Tindall, the Bethlem Hospital agent's wife, as matron. Those well on the way to recovery were allowed to visit people's homes. One night a lorry bringing patients failed to negotiate the right-angled turn over Salem Bridge, crashed through the railings and landed in the mud. Fortunately the river was low. No one was hurt, but raising the vehicle was a problem. Great shire horses were used in vain. One Sunday evening a crane arrived at the railway station and the usual crowd of small boys followed it to the bridge. It too failed. We missed the successful effort. A stream roller was at work on the road nearby and someone had the bright idea of linking it to the lorry. When the hospital was closed the beds were sold and my brother and I slept on two of them for years.

German prisoners of war worked on the neighbouring farms. They were billeted in the Conservative Working Men's Club. In the evening some of them could be seen sitting at open upstairs windows. A little boy called Wilson was often with them, a reminder of their own children. The Wilsons sold bread from a small shop near Westerman's. The latter became Barclay's Bank.

We saw Scottish troops, but I cannot remember whether it was whirling kilts or droning bagpipes that made us follow them on a route march. I remember just where on the Low Road to Friskney my small legs could march no more. Some of the nearby troops must have been mounted, for my father said that our stables would have been requisitioned if our yard had not been entered by a low narrow passage.

Most of our family went down with 'flu in the 1918 epidemic, and I had pneumonia. My parents said that they sat by my bed one night while a Zeppelin wandered overhead as if lost. I was still in bed when Mother, shedding tears of joy, came to tell me about the Armistice. I missed the immediate celebrations, but vaguely remember the varied empire and allied flags flown later. From this time I have two photographs taken by a Mr Smith in the yard behind Barton's shop. They show a goat and its cart. In the better picture Arthur Barton stands by the goat and in the cart are my sisters Ellen and Margaret. In the other faded picture is Jim Spence, son of a local auctioneer, wearing light clothes. The cart is decorated with flags. By it stands Ellen, while in the cart are my brother Sydney and myself.

The All Saints' War Memorial was made by Mr Woods, a local stonemason, and takes the form of an arch over the entrance to the public cemetery. I held Mother's hand during the dedication service, which was conducted by the Rector, Mr Hopkins, and the Wesleyan Minister, Mr Butters. Only when I read the story of Theodore Hardy, chaplain to the 8th Lincolns, did I realise how greatly that regiment suffered. In 1915, on the first day of the Battle of Loos the 8th Battalion lost half of its thousand men, and on the first day of the Battle of the Somme in 1919 it lost 251 men. A picture of volunteers taken at Lincoln shows men who remind me of the young farm hands whom I used to see. Their older brothers may have volunteered hoping to escape the monotony of their lives and unaware of what awaited them.

Local Defence Volunteers drilled on the Green Hill Field under the command of William Epton of Northolme Hall. Their armoury was in the office of Fred Waite who then kept a garage.

One Sunday teatime in 1919 or 1920 two Air Force officers came to our door. They had been to Skegness and their motor-cycle had broken down. They heard that my father had a car. Could he take them to Cranwell? He declined, but told them about Mr Waite. As they left our door my mother said, "Run after them and ask if they would like some tea". I caught them up at Cook's Corner. They accepted. Later father and we two small boys accompanied the officers to Mr Waite's. Sydney and I were given sixpence each for holding a torch while an inspection took place. Mr Waite then lent them a motor-cycle. Mrs Waite was sure that one of the officers was the Duke of York, later King George VI. We shall never know if she was right.

My sisters Ellen and Margaret, with Arthur Barton holding the goat

Peace Celebrations at Wainfleet

The author and his brother Sydney in the decorated goat cart,
with sister Ellen standing in front

The Louth Imp

Chapter 4

The Louth Imps

MANY of my Louth memories come from the time when, for almost seven years, I served under Canon H.P.W. Burton, an able man who was not sufficiently appreciated by the hierarchy of the Church of England.

Work began on restoring the spire of the Parish Church in 1937. It was entrusted to E. Bowman and Sons of Stamford. The Clerk of Works was Mr R.S. Godfrey, who had done such splendid work on Lincoln Cathedral. The estimated cost was £5,000, which was a large sum in those days. The appeal launched in October 1936 coincided with the 400th anniversary of the Louth Rebellion. I prefer the name Pilgrimage of Grace as the men involved were not really rebels at heart. They acted because of rumours that the parish churches would be despoiled as some of the monasteries had been. In a sermon at Evensong on that appeal Sunday I likened their march on Lincoln to those of the unemployed in and from the North-East of England in our time. But I added that in 1536 such protest meant crossing the will of the autocratic Henry VIII, gallows in the market place and a vicar dying a cruel death.

The spark that kindled the fire was the call of Thomas Foster on the fateful Sunday morning in 1536. He cried "Masters, let us follow the crosses this day. God knows whether we shall ever hereafter or nay". I was mildly amused to quote those words, for in the congregation was another Thomas Foster. He had been my housemaster when I was a boarder at the Grammar School and I became godfather to his daughter Daphne.

The Poor Law Institution in Louth was in process of changing slowly from Workhouse into County Hospital. As a schoolboy I had preached my first sermon in the Workhouse chapel. By 1936 what was then called the New Block had been built. I had taken a service there on that October morning. I told them that they would see scaffolding from their windows and spoke about the spire. When I finished, Miss Robinson, a good Methodist, called me to her bedside and put a shilling in my hand. The old age pension was ten shillings a week. Of this the inmates or patients kept just a shilling. That was one of the first contributions to the spire appeal fund.

My first climb on ladders through the scaffolding was made when they were not far short of the top of the spire. I was accompanied by Mr Arthur Ingram, a local builder, and Mr George Salisbury, Bowman's foreman. Arthur had once climbed up on steeplejack's ladders. The worst damage was on the north side and was partly caused by an unfortunate restoration in 1844, when the tower and spire had been struck by lightning. Hundreds of iron clamps had been used and these had rusted and eaten into the stonework. In some cases they had gone so deep that we should not have noticed them if Mr Salisbury had not pointed them out.

Few realised that there was scaffolding inside as well as outside the spire. That was necessary for the erection of a new needle post as the old one was rotten. It was replaced by one of oak and teak. Rustless delta bronze was used for strengthening.

Ascending the ladders made it possible to photograph details which are not easily seen from the ground. Thus on each face of the tower there is an imp which goes unnoticed because one does not think of looking for it.

On 9th July 1937 at 2.30 pm the big bell in the tower boomed to announce that the weathercock was about to be replaced. Two photographers from a national paper had come from Manchester for the occasion. They only went halfway, as there was a torrential downpour. Those who continued upwards were the Rector, his second daughter, Barbara, Mr Godfrey, Mr Salisbury, Mr J.P. Bowman, Mr Uzzel, representative of the Press, and myself. Miss Burton replaced the newly gilded bird on its perch. In the words of the Rector: "Then we were photographed, and a poor sodden group we were, but that did not matter, for it was our ambition to look workmanlike rather than beautiful".

It was the third cock to overlook the town. The first had begun as a basin which was part of the booty taken at the Battle of Flodden. It was bought in York and transformed in Lincoln.

. The climax of the thanksgiving for the restoration was a broadcast in June 1938. The preacher was the Bishop of Lincoln. During his sermon some of us had a few anxious moments. The church did not yet have electric lighting, and the Bishop had left his reading glasses at home; he resorted to a battery torch but lost his place in the script. There was what seemed to be, but perhaps was not, a long silence while he found his place. The sermon was too long and part of the Blessing as well as the whole of Owen Price's organ voluntary were lost. It is good, however, to have some record of that sermon. Speaking of the completion of the spire in 1515, the Bishop said: "Out of ordinary things and ordinary life had sprung this temporal sign of things Eternal. So their spire, like the Bible, was girt round with beauty. So had sprung from the levels of ordinary existence that which preached the grace of God. To the people of Louth he would say 'Look up at the Eternal Truth before you'; to others who perhaps knew no such spire, he wanted to say 'Look up and lift up your heads for your redemption draweth nigh'. ... Their church was the link between the seen and the unseen. Their spire, dwindling away from its foundations until it was lost in the sky, suggested a link with an unseen God."

No hard hats in 1937. John Swaby (L) with George Salisbury (Bowman's Foreman) and Alderman Blaze on the top platform. Left: the new weathercock in place

John holds tight to the single scaffold rail

The bedraggled party after replacing the weathercock on 9th July 1937. L-R: R.S. Godfrey, Canon Burton, Miss Barbara Burton, Mr Bowman jnr, Rev John Swaby and foreman George Salisbury.

My farewell in St James's Church in 1940. I am standing on the right. (Photo H.L. Howe)

Louth Spire

A wonder felt for nigh on eighty years is still
As fresh as February lambs,
Delight re-minted like the flowers of spring.
I mount a crest and suddenly I see
A little red roofed town that's built around
A stream that winding wanders from the hills.
Surmounting all there soars a coronet,
A spire majestic poetry in stone,
An ecstasy of music centuries old,
A skylark singing at it mounts aloft.
For fifteen years men strove to build this spire
And then with playing organs, clashing bells
They sang Te Deum in familiar words.
Te Deum too was wrought by craftsmen's hands.

We do not know the name of him who saw
The vision of proportions so exact,
Of him that dream of buttresses that fly
As if they're borne on wings of cherubim,
Strong tracery as delicate as lace,
A glory finely wrought in filigree.
Exultant praise here men have petrified.
The fire of joy in God burns in these stones.

Barkham Street in Wainfleet where I went to Florence Wilson's School

THE BROOK, SOMERSBY.

Chapter 5

Touches of Tennyson

PEOPLE living in Wainfleet, Louth, Mablethorpe and Barton on Humber may find a little interest in an account of how the life of a man whose life covered most of the 19th century has touched the life of one of whose life has covered most of the 20th.

My boyhood was spent in Wainfleet, but there was only one person I knew who ever mentioned the name of Alfred Tennyson. She was Florence Wilson, the dedicated teacher of small children at the Bryant School in Barkham Street. She gave me a copy of Tennyson's poetical works on my 21st birthday. She liked to think of Wainfleet as the 'little town' of 'The Brook'. There is, indeed, a watery link between Somersby and Wainfleet. The Somersby Brook enters the River Lymn which in the 12th century was diverted to join the stream carrying water from the East Fen to Wainfleet Haven. A more direct cut was made to the Haven in 1818. Of course the poet's description of a stream can be composite including features of several streams. The mention of 'twenty thorpes' and the fact that the poem was written soon after Tennyson left Somersby do, however, suggest that the Somersby Brook was at the front of his mind.

One might fancifully suggest that at Louth Grammar School the shadow of Tennyson fell on me at morning assembly where I stood beneath a bust of the poet. Three Tennyson brothers went to that school, residing with their grandmother in Westgate Place.

It is well known that Alfred was not happy at the school, and in later life he would not go down School House Lane. The headmaster Waite was a flogger, and it is interesting to note that the School's seal shows a bare-bottomed boy being caned. The school attended by Tennyson was on the same site as the one I attended. From the window one could see the old deep red brick garden wall of Westgate House with its foxgloves and a great variety of weeds. That wall was one of the few happy memories Alfred took away with him. I like to think that it inspired 'Flower in the Crannied Wall'.

> 'Flower in the crannied wall,
> I pluck you out of the crannies.
> I hold you here, root and all, in my hand.
> Little flower, but if I could understand
> What you are, root and all and all in all,
> I should know what God and man is.'

It is fancy on my part for the poem was written fifty years after Tennyson left Louth and crannied walls are plentiful. I do however confess to beginning a Harvest Festival sermon in Louth St James as if fancy were fact.

At Mablethorpe, where I was rector from 1953 to 1960, the poet was inescapable. The children of Rector Tennyson often spent holidays there and I read with delight a letter in the County Archives from the exasperated Rector when he found he was late in booking rooms, "Every shed in Mablethorpe, Sutton and Trusthorpe is occupied by greasy and pot-bellied grocers and linen drapers".

The story is well known of how Alfred and his brother Charles hired a carriage to go from Somersby to Mablethorpe to shout their verses to the waves after Jackson of Louth had printed *Poems by Two Brothers*.

Tennyson continued to visit the little place and loved it to the end of his life. The population of St Mary's parish was 205 in 1841. St Peter's parish had 37. White's Directory of 1842 said there were about a dozen lodging houses in addition to the Book in Hand. A grocer, bricklayer, coal merchant, fishermen, carrier and gardener took in summer guests. The gardener was George Wildman and Sir Charles Tennyson, the poet's grandson and biographer, quotes from a letter Tennyson wrote to his future wife in 1839. "I am housed at Mr Wildman's, an old friend of mine in these parts. He and his wife are two perfectly honest Methodists. When I came I asked his wife after news and she replied, 'Why Mr Tennyson, there's only one piece of news that I know, that Christ died for all men'. I said to her, 'that is the old news and goods news and new news', wherewith she seemed to be satisfied."

Not long before the poet's death, his son visited Somersby, Mablethorpe and Bayon's Manor and reported to his father how

The bay-windowed house on the right was one of the places where the Tennysons had seaside lodgings

The lonely cottage behind "a sand built ridge of heaped hills that mound the sea"

they fared. A planned visit by Sir Charles to Mablethorpe had to be cancelled as no one seemed interested in the subject. I knew that one house where Tennyson had stayed was behind Mr Jackson's amusement arcade near the Pullover. What I did discover was that the fireplace surround of one house in Mablethorpe had had tiles depicting scenes from Tennyson's poems, and I was able to send a few to the Tennyson collection in the Usher Art gallery in Lincoln.

No one has better described the incoming tide on this part of Lincolnshire coast than Tennyson did, likening the fall of a knight in 'The Last Tournament' to

> Fall as the crest of some slow arching wave
> Heard in the dead of night along that table shore,
> Drops flat, and after the great waters break
> Whitening for half a league and thin themselves
> Far over sands marbled with moon and cloud,
> From less and less to nothing.

John Betjeman recited those words in his inimitable way at a meeting in Louth Town Hall of the Lincolnshire Old Churches Trust.

'Ode to Memory' was one of Tennyson's earliest poems and clearly refers to the Lincolnshire coast.

> .... a sand built ridge
> Of heaped hills that mound the sea,
> Overblown with murmurs harsh,
> Or even a lonely cottage whence we see
> Stretch'd wide and wild the waste enormous marsh.

I was vicar of Barton on Humber from 1960 to 1971 and Tennyson pursued me even there. The Tennysons had lived across the Humber in Yorkshire before they came to Lincolnshire. Sir Charles discovered that a Ralph Tennyson had been articled to a Barton solicitor, so the Tennyson Society held a meeting in the town. Unfortunately little could be seen of the house where Ralph Tennyson had lived on the south side of the Market Place; a newsagent's shop had been built in the front of it.

Soon after the visit, I made two discoveries. The first was that R. Brown, author of a two volume book of *The Early History of Barton on Humber*, wrote an ode in the poet's memory on Tennyson's death. The second was the discovery among thrown away rubbish in a dusty cupboard in St Peter's church vestry of a musical setting of 'Crossing the Bar'. It was in the early version of *Hymns Ancient and Modern* but has been omitted from later revisions. The only time I sang it was at the funeral of a Humber pilot.

The hymn 'Strong son of God, Immortal love' still appears in new editions of *The English Hymnal*. It is based on the preface to 'In Memoriam'.

There are times when I wonder what I would have said if I had been able to accept an invitation to preach at the annual service of the Tennyson Society. Few poets have had the same quality of music in their work as Tennyson, and the combination of poetry and music appeals to the human heart at deep levels. What, however, I think should have spoken about would have been the fact that Tennyson had a mind well equipped to deal with the controversies of his day, controversies which made people doubt their faith.

It is worth noting that 'In Memoriam' appeared ten years before *The Origin of Species*, and that in the years between the early death of Arthur Hallam in 1833 and the publication of 1849 the poet was wrestling with such problems as

> Are God and Nature then at strife
> That Nature lends such ideal dreams?
> So careful of the type she seems
> So careless of the single type.
>
> So careful of the single type, but no,
> From scarred cliff and from quarried stone
> She cries 'A thousand types are gone
> I care for nothing, all shall go'.

Yet for all of his doubts and questions, Tennyson believed that the love such as he had for his friend pointed to Reality. He may have been an infant crying in the night, but he cried as one who knows his father is near.

In a book published in 1933, C.S. Carpenter wrote of the work of scholars in resisting what was a confident rejection of Christianity. He then told how they had allies in the 'amateur theologians'. One of these was Tennyson. These played their part in restoring the figure of Christ to the centre of the picture. When the work had been done it was no longer possible to pass Him by. They dispersed the mists by which an unthinking religiousity had surrounded Him, they stripped off the grave clothes with which the so-called Rationalists were proposing to endue Him. They put before the

19th century the inspiring challenging question 'What think ye of Christ?' And Tennyson was one who cried 'Ring in the Christ that is to be.' I end by again quoting from 'In Memoriam':

> And so the Word had breath and wrought
>   With human hands the creed of creeds
>   In loveliness of perfect deeds
> More strong than all poetic thought.

Arching waves break on the table shore, as Tennyson evoked in
'The Last Tournament'

Chapter 6

Scunthorpe St John's Church

I WAS vicar of Scunthorpe from late 1940 to April 1953. Although St John's Church served the purpose for which it was erected for less than a century, it was not an inglorious story. To many people the name Scunthorpe means the borough as a whole, but the original Scunthorpe was just one of the five constituent townships. Each was a narrow strip partly on the ridge known as the Cliff and partly below it in the Trent valley. Danish Ashby was in the ecclesiastical parish of Saxon Bottesford while Danish Brumby, Scunthorpe and Crosby were in the ecclesiastical parish of Saxon Frodingham.

The place name Scunthorpe probably derives from the man Skuma, but I am biased in favour of a word that has to do with 'esk' or water. (The Domesday book version starts with 'escum'.) A subterranean stream runs down the High Street, occasionally appearing in the cellars of shops. It may have ended in a pond near the church, and it may not be coincidence that when the pond was filled in, two feet of water appeared in the heating chamber of the church. That was my introduction to the parish, and for my first winter the church was heated by two small borrowed stoves with their chimneys stuck through windows. Eventually, after much argument, we managed to drain into a sewer, although water had still to be channelled inside the chamber.

In 1832 there were just over 600 people in the ecclesiastical parish of Frodingham and 249 of them were in the Scunthorpe part. Change began in the middle of the century when ironstone was found on the land of Rowland Winn, later Lord St Oswald. Until then the east end of the townships had been waste where thousands of geese were raised, walked through tar and sand to shod them, and then driven to London. By 1882 Scunthorpe had two thousand inhabitants and in 1890 Edmund Akenhead took charge of a new parish consisting of Scunthorpe and Crosby. Being a man with grand ideas he had a very large vicarage, with three acres of grounds, on Normanby Road, far away from the church. The schools in Gurnell Street appeared. Incidentally it was impossible for me to live in the huge vicarage as I had no private income and a large slice of my income provided a pension for my predecessor.

On 15 April 1891 Edward King, Bishop of Lincoln, consecrated the church, the gift of Lord St Oswald. Appropriately the building rested on slag balls. Above ground it was ironstone faced with Ancaster stone. When the peer died in 1893, seven bells were added to the original one, making the only eight bell peal in the area. At that time there is no doubt that the east end of Scunthorpe was the most important in what is now a borough. The railway station, post office, library, police station and council offices were there.

In Henry Richard Ashdown's time, 1898-1909, the population of the parish doubled. In the time of Thomas Boughton it reached fifteen thousand and the vicar had three curates, a lady worker and a stipendiary reader to assist him. Curates were expected to wear silk top hats. In 1919 Crosby became a separate ecclesiastical district.

In the same year Mr C.J. Turrell began his memorable work at Santon, right amongst the steel works, partly in Scunthorpe and partly in Appleby. The mission church of St Nicholas was opened in 1921, but unfortunately the site was wanted for ironstone mining in 1937. In conjunction with the vicar of Appleby we started a Sunday School in borrowed premises. The Rev. Arthur Muxlow did good work there. As for Mr Turrell, I think that in his loyal and quiet way he did as much, if not more, good than some of the town clergy have done.

In Canon Steele's time the numbers in the parish grew rapidly, but most of that growth was far from the church and most of the people were nearer other churches. Tradesmen, for the most part, ceased to live over their shops. Paralysis was creeping up the High Street. I was told three disused chapels had been sold in one day. By 1960 even the great Trinity Methodist Church had been replaced by a Home Store.

To meet the expansion below the Cliff a site was bought in the parish which would serve the lower end of three parishes, but the outbreak of war prevented the erection of a building. When the time to build came after I had left, it was found that someone else had built on the site. He was compelled to find an alternative site on which the Church of the Resurrection was built.

THE PARISH CHURCH, SCUNTHORPE

K 5436

V. 72-2. Interior, Scunthorpe Church

My ministry in Scunthorpe started with the discomfort of a cold church. At the end we had to sing to a piano. The three manual organ, best in the town, needed attention. The organist of York Minster suggested as clerk of works a man who knew a lot about the practical side of organ building and he recommended a firm he knew. The clerk of works died. Letters produced no result, nor did visits to the organ builder. Later he went bankrupt and it became evident that he had used parts of our organ to repair others.

Nor was it easy going in between the cold beginning and the organless ending. Perhaps in a patriotic gesture, and maybe also because the Church was overdrawn at the bank, the Church Hall had been let for the Ministry of Food. We needed it. The Borough Council let us have the old Library for youth work on most generous terms, but we badly needed the Hall. It took seven years to get it back. That we succeeded was due mainly to our Member of Parliament, Mr E.L. Mallalieu. The Food people had to go, as we had long suggested, to the old Library.

Soon after I went to Scunthorpe an uncle had said, "A nice Church, but down town". A cleric who shall be nameless, referring to the verger seeking a better job, spoke of rats leaving a sinking ship. The people of St John's never regarded it as such. They might be down town but they were not down-hearted.

One afternoon will give an idea of how varied life could be. I took the funeral of a member of the congregation who had been murdered, went from the cemetery to take a wedding, and then on to the police station to see photographs. The Scotland Yard men thought I might know how the victim would react to certain situations.

After the brief ministry of my successor the people received a series of blows. The diocese seemed determined to kill the parish. It was kept vacant for two years while two commissions met and rejected suggestions to re-absorb the parish in Frodingham. When appointments were made two of the four incumbents had other jobs. The second job of one was in Germany. Finally, as once Scunthorpe St John's had included Crosby so now Crosby absorbed St John's. I cannot forget the comment of Hadyn Williams, warden for between thirty and forty years, "They closed my church and took away much of my life". There were still four thousand people in the parish when the church was closed and I cannot help thinking of what John Milton wrote in Lycidas: "The hungry sheep look up and are not fed".

What depressed me when I returned was to see old streets replaced by tower blocks of flats. The old streets were friendly. The V.E. celebrations made that plain, although I did find that three street parties in one day put a strain on the digestion. Princess Street, a cul de sac with an unmade road and water supplied to outdoor taps, was the best decorated in the borough. A man who spent his boyhood in one of those old streets and loved St John's summed it up: "The standard of life is better now. The quality of life was better then".

The second part of the poem 'Ghosts of Memory' (see inside back cover) expresses my feelings about the old East End of the parish.

Some thought that I would stay in Scunthorpe for the rest of my full-time ministry, but after more than twelve years I was very tired. Canon Burton in his retirement wrote, "I had plenty to do; even today the clergy in that town work incessantly from early morning to late at night. Had one or two of the clergy whom I knew been preferred to other places after a few years in that town they might have gone from strength to strength; they need more leisure for thought, study and extra-parochial concerns. It is surprising that many of our leaders attained to high office among the more pleasant paths".

There was certainly little spare time. My *History of Louth* was not published until twelve years after I promised to write it. For two years nothing was written. Nearly all was written after ten at night.

In April 1941 the Bishop of Lincoln had come for the celebration of the Golden Jubilee of the consecration of St John's. In April 1951 the Bishop of Grimsby came to preach in the morning and Canon Burton in the evening as we kept the Diamond Jubilee. I had no idea that within a little over a year I should be thinking about leaving Scunthorpe. I had not thought of it until I was asked to consider going to another large steel town parish – Attercliffe in Sheffield. There were fifty thousand people, four churches and three or four curates. I asked the Bishop of Lincoln for advice and he thought I needed to ease up a bit. He suggested the possibility of Mablethorpe. Before the decision was taken the flood of 31st January 1953 occurred. So I went to Mablethorpe. I have sometimes wondered if I shirked the challenge of Attercliffe.

concluded on page 46

A Dream

(Scunthorpe)

Some years ago I dreamed that I was dead.
I saw a column coming up the road
Of goodly knights and sturdy marching men;
Their flags and pennons fluttered in the breeze,
The spears and lances glittered in the sun,
The warrior hosts of God returning home.
The fortress city gates were opened wide;
The people crowded towers and battlements,
Triumphant trumpets sounded golden notes.
I read the names of banners raised aloft –
The names of places that I knew so well –
Of Lincoln, Durham, Louth and Messingham.
Others had names with no familiar ring
Like Aklavik, Dogura and Sabah.
A second column soon appeared in sight
And in the distant dust a third was seen.
These thrilling sights had filled my heart and joy,
But as the shadows lengthened I grew sad.
There were some faithful servants of our King
Who loved one house of God within their town.
And were distressed when worship ceased
And they were scattered far and wide.
I knew them well and I had shared their pain.
The armies now were safe within the walls;
The trumpets ceased; the daylight fainter grew;
A silence wrapped around the scene and me.
It seemed that it might never have an end
Until a piercing shattering cry arose
From those still watching on the ramparts tall.
With glad abandonment they cried 'They come'.
It was a band of 'Old Contemptibles'
Which marched like weary men who came from Mons
Or from the blasted beaches of Dunkirk.

The men who felt the heat of furnace fires,
Women who'd cared for others till they dropped,
The teachers from the Day and Sunday Schools,
The workers from the offices and shops,
The denizens of older, poorer streets,
The humble folk no history records,
The ones who did kind deeds asking no praise,
The boys who often went with me to camp.
I saw my brother limp with damaged hip.
He looked at me with smiles and raised his hand.
And Taffy Williams grasped the friendly arm
Of one beside him. He was blind.
All these had come. Their tattered banner high
Proclaimed ST JOHN'S. And now once more in joy
The churches' bells crashed out and fanfares rang.
I saw a sort of college dining hall,
Long tables and the benches black with age
And lit by torches flaming near the walls.
A dais was there, a mighty log fire burned.
These victors had no drunken revelry.
The knights of God had helmets by their plates.
They were at ease and yet not unprepared
As those who still might have more work to do.
Now they all rise to toast their Lord and King.
A swelling chorus like huge rollers broke
Upon shield dotted walls and timbered roof:
THE VICTORY IS TO OUR GOD ENTHRONED
AND TO THE LAMB.

I do not consider myself as one of Canon Burton's 'one or two'. I think I was meant to be an ordinary parish priest. I am grateful, however, that my job has taken me to such a variety of places – market and industrial towns, seaside and Humberside, villages in Wold and Marsh. Sometimes I wonder if I was not being led towards Barton on Humber for an ecumenical venture.

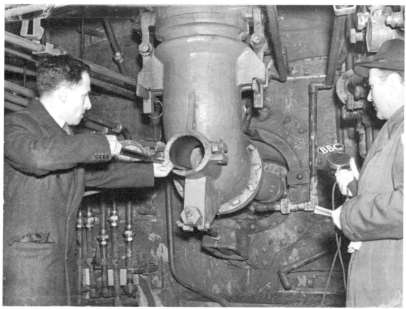

In 1952 the author was invited to restart the giant Appleby-Frodingham steel furnace following maintenance and re-lining

Chapter 7

Memories of Mablethorpe

I WAS rector of Mablethorpe from early 1953 to late 1960. Mablethorpe St Mary's has been likened to a Viking longboat with high prow and stern. The chancel is higher than the tower. The local story is that the rector, responsible for the chancel, carried out repairs and the people conveniently forgot their duty.

I accepted the benefice without seeing the church. The resignation of my predecessor who lived five miles away, took effect on 31st January 1953, the night when the sea defences broke. When I came to look round I reached the edge of the town. Great machinery was moving in to plug gaps. So I turned back, not to be a nuisance. In any case most of the people had been evacuated.

One of the unseen and undecorated heroes of that night was the Rev. Mr Josey, Methodist minister. Long hours spent in deep cold water rescuing people damaged his health.

Automatically I took charge of Stain, which had been united with St Mary's in 1662. It had one house. I was also vicar of Theddlethorpe All Saints' and rector of St Helen's with Mablethorpe St Peter's. My list of titles reminds me of Dr Smyth, the *Church Times* had fun over my appointment, suggesting that a bathing costume would be appropriate for induction to St Peter's – it had been under the sea for more than four hundred years. It received its first battering in 1287, and it would seem that the church of St Mary was rebuilt farther inland soon afterwards. It is said that Marshall Hayley had predicted the 1953 storm and no one knew that shore better than he did. He took visitors for boat rides, caught crabs, and it was his beachcombing activities that caused Mablethorpe to be listed as a place of Roman settlement. When the Duke of Edinburgh came on the completion of the new sea walls, Hayley presented him with a Roman relic. Hayley was a man of very fixed opinions and it was impossible to convince him that Mablethorpe St Peter's had ever existed. In spite of ample documentary evidence and known

St Mary's Church, Mablethorpe

boundaries shown on maps he held that all references were to Trusthorpe St Peter's.

On the day the Duke was expected I had a journey on treacherous icy roads to Louth to take a funeral. On my return I was told that the Duke's plane could not land at Manby because of the weather. The luncheon provided by the Council had to go on. The Duke came the next week and we had another meal at the Council's expense.

Among the councillors was Mr Brownlow, a retired Lincoln grocer. To see him pushing an old pram around and to see junk that littered his front garden might make one think of Steptoe and Son. That would be to misjudge him. He collected and sold scrap, but he kept none of the proceeds of sales for himself. In the war he collected enough to build a Spitfire. Then he built a shelter on the sea front. This annoyed some of the amusement caterers as rain drove the trippers to seek protection in their arcades. In my time there he provided a Christmas dinner for lonely people.

> I wonder if in deepest dead of night
> The shade of Brownlow's pram will haunt the street,
> And squeal 'O spare a passing thought for him
> the man who sometimes made you smile
> But had the power to warm the human heart.'

There was a time when the Tennysons of Somersby and the Brackenbury's of Raithby Hall had long stays in the summer. Later there were specialised boarding houses but the stays were shorter. In my time Mablethorpe was very much a place for day trippers. Even so it was possible to find the beach, washed twice in 24 hours by the sea, empty about eight in the morning and I would take my small daughter and the dog with me to gather driftwood. Her first sledge was made from a washed-up fish box. The season lasted for only about nine weeks and in that time people had to make enough to last them through the winter. One family I knew lived in the garage and let their house during the season.

In 1953 there was no season and much time was spent in hearing claims for relief. Once, by chance, two other clerics and myself formed the hearing panel. The claimant looked at us and said, "Parsons know nothing about business". The accountant sent by Birmingham City Council intervened. "How is it that the figures in your claim are so much higher than those stated in your income tax returns for the last year?" The man grinned and said, "I think I'd better drop my claim". Most claims were genuine and treated as such.

*Ole Gooden, the parish clerk, from a mid-19th century
painting by J.W. Wilson, solicitor, Louth*

The rectory, which had been near the church, had been burnt down centuries earlier and absentee rectors paid curates to do their work and pocketed what remained. When I came to Empingham in 1984 I found that Lovick Cooper, who had been rector there for fifty years, had held Mablethorpe in plurality. Happily for Mablethorpe one curate was James Quarmby. When he died the paper, presumably the *Stamford Mercury*, described him as 'The Friend of the Children'. He started a Sunday School and then a Day School in a barn. When he died his body was buried in the chancel of the church, but when that part of the church was tiled his memorial was covered up. The brasses of the Fitzwilliams, who once lived at the Hall, were preserved and are now in the wall at the east end of the north aisle.

Mr Whitelaw was probably the first resident incumbent for centuries. He too lived at the Hall. His daughter told a delightful story about him. One Sunday his sermon was long and a visitor made a show of consulting his watch. Whereupon the rector produced his: "I make the time so and so. What do you?"

She also told of a farmer named Wood, the son of a former vicar of Theddlethorpe All Saints. One day he read the parable told by Nathan about a rich man with many flocks of sheep and a poor man with one little ewe lamb. (2 Samuel Ch.1). A visitor was greatly puzzled by the Lincolnshire pronunciation of the word ewe and enquired afterwards, "What is a yow?"

The picture of Ole Gooden, the parish clerk had been painted by James William Wilson of Louth and given to me by Mr W.A. Slack, a Louth solicitor. His firm had handled affairs of the Wilson family. I was able to hand it to the old man's descendants who were called Gooding.

One day a military historian came to see me. He was interested in an army officer called Jolland who, I think, had served in India. He wanted to find Jolland's watch which for some reason had come into the hands of the Wilson family. He was looking for Miss Wilson, but she had left Mablethorpe. On his return home he wrote to tell me that he learned from a taxi driver that a Miss Wilson had just gone into hospital. It was the lady he wanted and he went to see her. Unfortunately some naughty relative had sold the watch.

31 January 1953

High springs the spindrift
Whirled o'er the sea wall;
Loud booms the wave crash
Thudding like thunder;
Woeful the wind wail
Screeching in torment;
Awful the howling
Threnody threatful.

Beaches are flayed bare,
Stripped to the clay bone;
Sandhills erode fast;
Concrete is smashed up,
Broken like egg shells;
Night of the wind's might.
Terror and turmoil.

Rollers race inland
Through breached defences.
Like panzer storm troops
Nothing can stop them.
Old ones are 'prisoned,
Trapped in low dwellings,
Held by the flood hordes,
Frail and bewildered.

Rescuers reach them,
Waist deep in water,
Carry the aged.
Through the wild wilderness
Unto the transports,
To warmth and shelter
In distant places.

Sand like a serpent
Slides into houses,
Glides into gutters,
Coils into gardens.
Salt crusts the pastures,
Salt cakes the ploughlands,
Seeps into tree roots
Doomed soon the wither.

Lorries in convoys.
Cranes in procession,
Slag loads from Scunthorpe,
Bulldozers, forklifts
Fill up the Marsh roads,
Facing to plug gaps
Ere the next high tide
Brings fresh disasters.

Steel piles in hundreds
Rammed in the sea bed,
Mountains of concrete
Poured into sea walls,
Make new defences
League upon league long.
People return now.
Mablethorpe lives on.

*The Duke of Edinburgh visited Sutton and Mablethorpe
in the wake of the 1953 flood (Photo: Grimsby Telegraph)*

Chapter 8

Thunder over the Wold

IN HIS poem 'A Lincolnshire Church', John Betjeman described how the thunder 'greyly tremendous' hung over the width of the Wold, but the green Marsh was unclouded. On a 'gentle eminence' the church tower was 'silver and brown in the sunlight'.

Many years ago I preached in that church. After the service the Anglo-Indian vicar said, "I am sorry that I cannot ask you to supper. My wife is ill". It was plain that he too was ill. A few days later my wife, small daughter and I walked up a muddy path to the vicarage to enquire about the old couple. We entered a kitchen with a coke stove that heated and clouded it with dust. It was a sad scene of failing health and poverty. The vicar was lying on a couch. That night he died. We heard that he was very fond of children, and that our daughter's visit had made his last hours happy. The widow left the district and died not long afterwards. To our surprise she had left Sara a small legacy that was large by the standards of those with little to spare.

The scene comes to mind as one thinks of Henry Robling, rector of Gayton le Wold, poor, ill and dying as the thunder hung 'greyly tremendous' over wold and marsh alike. His wife had predeceased him and he was tended by his unmarried daughters Rachel and Mary.

When Robling went to Gayton in 1613 it was to a dying village. There were a dozen houses in it by 1640 and in the next century only three.

> .... trembling from the spoiler's hand,
> Far, far away, thy children leave the land.

The rectory in three quarters of an acre of land was also in decay. It had started as a two-roomed dwelling consisting of a hall, which was both sitting and dining room, and a parlour for sleeping. All was on one level. By 1606 it had spread laterally to five bays. By 1630 two chambers had been added above the parlour.

The framework of the house was wood infilled with earth. The ground floors were of beaten earth and those of the chambers were of puddled clay laid on reeds which had been placed across the joist. The roof was thatched. It was a typical parsonage of the period and resembled the dwelling of a wealthier yeoman. It needed constant repair and by the end of the period only the wild waste of a garden marked the site. The house was non-existent, the parson non-resident.

The glebe was only a little arable in Grimblethorpe and two pastures in the west, down by the river Bain. These were lost soon after Robling's death in 1650. He himself seems to have had rights in the distant fen which provided good summer grazing for horses and cattle. As the benefice was a rectory, the incumbent received both greater and lesser tithes but even so it was worth only £30 a year, which put it on a level with the "very great number of very poore and miserable vicarages" that Archbishop Laud reported were in Lincolnshire. Over eighty per cent of the benefices in the county fell below the £80 or £100 a year, which the Committee of Plunder Ministers, set up by Parliament in December 1643, considered adequate.

The Committee had at its disposal the revenues of the old Church hierarchy and a number of 'impropriate' rectories sequestered from Royalists and Roman Catholics. An 'impropriate' rectory was usually one from which a lay rector took the greater tithes. In February 1647 Robling was granted £50 a year from the impropriate rectory of Girsby sequestered from the Roman Catholic William Compton, but money voted in London did not come easily into a Gayton pocket. It was discovered that the Girsby money had been allocated to someone else. In April 1647 a new order was made. The sequestrators were to pay Robling £50 p.a. from the impropriate rectory of Nun Ormsby sequestered from the delinquent Souths of Kelstern and £20 p.a. from the impropriate rectory of Little Grimsby sequestered from the recusant Mrs Aprice. But problems remained. In June 1649 the Souths compounded for their delinquency, and not only did the Nun Ormsby £50 cease to be available for Gayton, but the Souths evaded the payment of arrears. So when Robling made his will he left his children the proceeds "if anything can be gotten and received of my augmentation money granted and due to me from Nun Ormsby".

The will was witnessed by Henry Strelley, rector of Withcall and proved in 1650. "I commend my soul into the hands of Almighty God who before the foundation of the world was layd did of his free mercy elect me to salvation, whereby his only Son, Jesus Christ, my alone Saviour, did redeem me from everlasting death, and by his blessed Spirit did seale unto me the earnest of everlasting inheritance, saying unto my soul I am thy salvation". Robling left £1 to Henry, his eldest son, £3 to John, £6 to Thomas and £7 to his daughter Anne, wife of Richard Caswell of London. The remainder went to Rachel and Mary.

On Robling's death an inventory of his goods and chattels was made. His was a simple furnished home. His purse and apparel were valued at £3 and the hall furniture at the same sum. The parlour and upper chambers contained three beds, one being a trundle bed that could be pushed under another when not in use, two chests, a coffer and an old trunk, a few boxes, some loose boards and two strikes of malted barley. The contents of the kitchen were valued at £1 6s 8d and of the dairy at 6s.

The contents of the little farm were worth more than those of the house. A haystack in the yard made up of four loads was worth £1 6s 8d, a bay mare £5 10s, three fillies in the fen £9, geese and other pullen at 5s, three cows and a calf £10, 23 sheep £6 and four swine £2. The total of £49 was less than that of the average clerical inventory of the period.

We can picture Robling as a shabbily dressed man with muddy boots. His hands are hardened by outdoor toil, his face weather beaten, his brow much wrinkled by the worry of supporting six children. His family knew all about living on fat bacon and pickled onions, helped out by vegetables from the garden, eggs from its own chickens and a rabbit snared on the waste. Like many other families they made their own bread, ale and cheese. When the uncertain augmentations came in it was too late. Some of the fledglings had left the nest and Robling's life was nearly over.

The hours that Robling kept were measured by the sun. How did he spend them? He would read prayers daily in the church, visit the parishioners and, after the Book of Homilies was banned, laboriously prepare a sermon. Sometimes he would ride the bay mare into Louth, stable the beast at the White Swan or the Saracen's Head and listen to local gossip over a mug of ale. He might visit relatives in the town or wander round the market where Gayton folk could buy and sell without paying toll. He might even attend the weekday lecture on which Puritans set great store. It was sometimes delivered by his friend Strelley. He might ride another day to see the fillies in the fen, but most of his days would be spent in tending his few other beasts and tilling his land. In addition to teaching his children how to milk a cow or shear a sheep, and he may also have had a hand in the more literary part of their education. He seems to have read little, for no books are mentioned in his inventory, but that omission may be because the man who compiled the list did not know what to make of books.

In the reign of Henry VIII a storm had raged over the Wolds and Robert Benson, one of the Robling's predecessors, had been lucky to escape with his life after taking part in the Lincolnshire Pilgrimage of Grace. When skies were black in the reign of Charles I, Robling and his people were less dramatic in their reaction to change. Archbishop Laud ordered that the Holy Table be placed permanently at the east end of the chancel. They complied. Parliament ordered that the railings be taken away. They obeyed. To older men like Robling this was a return to a practice to which they had been accustomed throughout most of their ministries.

When Civil War broke out, Williamson of Saltfleetby All Saints, a keen Royalist, rode about with Cavaliers, waving a sword and brandishing a pistol. On the other hand Mawer of Muckton said the Queen was a whore and her children bastards. These men were exceptions. Most of the clergy in the area kept their heads down.

Life became more difficult when Parliament banned the Prayer Book and ordered the Directory of Public Worship substituted, but orders made in London could be ignored in remote places. There were more parishes that kept the old book than those which bought the new. Moreover the Directory was only a series of aids to Do-It-Yourself worship. If there were no busybodies around the old and familiar could be retained. Only enough changes needed to be made to keep the letter of the law.

The men who acted thus were not all Vicars of Bray, intent on retaining their livings at all costs. Many had a sense of pastoral responsibility and saw no point in making gestures that only got them ejected and left the people to the mercy of the fanatics.

I knew a 20th century rector of Gayton le Wold. He too had children to support on a small income. He was passed over for preferment, but he never lost his Welsh fervour. Week by week he gave of his best in this and two other Wold parishes. He could afford new books, but he valued what he had.

We do not know if his 17th century predecessor gave of his best to his few people. We should dearly like to have a few letters or a diary to show where his sympathies were in the conflicts of the time. He may have only wanted to be left alone. Whatever be the truth in the case of a particular individual, it is true to say that the Church of England came through the mid-17th crisis because of the labours of many moderate and obscure rural ministers. Because of them the Church, its worship and its buildings gained a 'gentle eminence' in the hearts of common folk. Like Betjeman's tower, that Church was brown with a certain earthiness and also silver with sunlight. It was as muddy as Robling's boots and as bright as the faith expressed in his last will and testament.

Chapter 9

A Heave of Churchyards

THE collective noun was suggested by Gray's 'Elegy in a Country Churchyard' in which he writes "Beneath the rugged elms and yew tree's shade, Where heaves the turf in many a mouldering heap".

Gray was not in my mind. On that day one heard no curfew bell or lowing herd winding across the leas. There was only the cacaphony of murdered and mutilated music or the bellow of loud speakers inviting us to join the knobbly knees competition for the honour of Gloucester House. I was at a Clergy Conference in Butlin's Holiday Camp. There was one consolation. Ingoldmells was not far from my boyhood home. So I decided to go on a churchyard crawl in Wainfleet.

I did not go to indulge in nostalgia by reading the names on gravestones of those known in days gone by, although I had had the humiliating experience of returning to old haunts to find that as few of the living remembered me as remembered Rip Van Winkle when he went home after his long sleep. A new generation had arisen that knew not Joseph.

I wished to rectify an omission. Often there are places on the doorstep that you mean to see tomorrow, but proverbially tomorrow never comes. I had often entered the public cemetery through the Arc de Tristesse et Gloire that the local stonemason had erected as a war memorial, traversed the graveyard around the new All Saints and stood beside graves in the well-kept churchyard of the lonely and lovely St Mary's. But there were yet three more burial grounds that I had never entered. Perhaps I might find something to make the journey worthwhile.

The public cemetery adjoins St Thomas's graveyard. This small area of raised ground is called Northolme. It was once an island near the mouth of the river and not far from the Green Hill on which a beacon burned to guide ships into harbour. A man once said, "The King of the boggarts is in there and if he gets out it will take all the parsons in the Marsh a month of Sundays to get him in again".

Imagination took charge. I saw a crumbling cottage long gone, whitewashed and thatched. Some of its stones may have come from the chapel of St Thomas of Canterbury. Sober clad General Baptists were walking to worship through the keck. They were allowed use of the chapel during the Commonwealth. Was the river used for baptisms? Did Robert Shalders of Croft come here? When he died in 1666 the Anglicans of Croft showed their loyalty to the old order by digging up his body and dragging it on a sledge to his house. Bearded Dutchmen came to burn to rob and sail away.

The Augustinians of Kyme had charge of the chapel of the 'Blissful martyr'. Here they convalesced in the sea breezes or recovered from the annual blood letting then regarded as the panacea of all bodily ills. In the 15th century the resident monks were in trouble for preferring to live in separate seaside cottages rather than in the common boarding house. There had been wild doings on the Eve of All Saints' in 1298. A renegade priest led a party of vandals trying to wreck the building the remains of which was now beneath my feet. So the Bishop ordered the Rural Dean of Candleshoe to have the sentence of excommunication read at Mass 'with bells ringing and candles burning' in the churches of Wainfleet and around.

Doubtless I could have conjured up these pictures elsewhere, but on that day they came spontaneously. It was as if the spirit of the place affected me. Then, as the dream faded and I was about to slip between the bars of the boundary fence, I saw a stone in memory of the man who a century earlier ran the business which my father had done. He had lived where I had lived. So for a moment one felt forcibly the links between the present and the past.

The new All Saints' church was erected in 1821. The old church was near the bank which had held back the flooded waters of the East Fen. The first settlement had been on that piece of high ground between the morass and the sea. As the sea receded so did the people, and in the end the church followed them. In the 18th century the old church had been improved by the hanging of five heavy bells. In consequence the tower sank and the nave lurched. When other bells rang throughout England to celebrate the victory of Trafalgar those bells were silent. By the time the Battle of Waterloo was fought the church was unused.

When the old church was pulled down there was a piece of iconoclasm that surprises our more heritage conscious age. One would have thought that the local people would have venerated the man who built for their forefathers a school in 1484, and revelled in the story of how

> 'Oft in the marsh beneath a level sun
> He sought with crook his father's sheep,
> Or, boyish, traced his Magdalene in the sand.' *(H.D.Rawnsley)*

William of Wainfleet had made good. He became Lord Chancellor of England and founded an Oxford College, but in the early 19th century Oxford was worlds away. Even today few people have an historical sense and fewer still can romanticise with Rawnsley. In 1831 they simply smashed the tomb that William had erected to his father, 'breaking the carved work with axes and hammers'.

I knew from a tablet in the new All Saints that the President and Scholars of Magdalen College had caused a memorial to be placed on the site in the old churchyard. So on that warm afternoon churchyard I waded through the knee high grass to find it. Knowing the tomb had been in the south choir, I knew where the old church had been.

I did not find the grave of May Grebby, the old sexton, 'who going home on the Saturday night, it being dark and stormy, missed his way and was found dead on the Sunday morning, Easter Day 1781'.

Not far way, in the parish of St Mary, is the land that John Baldock left as a burial ground for himself, his family and 'the people called Quakers'. It is well disguised. There is no heaving turf. There are no monuments. On that day it was the graveyard of a derelict car, and yet

> 'Perchance in this neglected place is laid
> Some heart once pregnant with celestial fire.'

Here in 1769 the Quakers laid to rest the body of a man whose ancestors were Huguenot refugees. At the age of nine he was apprenticed to a weaver and became known as William the Weaver. About 1772 he set up in Wainfleet as a grazier and wool merchant. In 1742 he began his travels as a missionary. From America he had written, "notwithstanding all the censures, evil surmisings and reproaches that have been or may be cast upon me, I have a great peace in what I believe to be my duty". His surname was Reckitt, and his descendants have become famous for their philanthropy as well as for their starch and blue.

This churchyard crawl provided the setting for a little meandering in the paths of local history. It made clearer the fact that almost every acre of England has a story worth telling. It shows that things of interest can be unseen until we almost trip over them. But since that visit the question has come to me again and again, "Why seek ye the living among the dead?" The churchyards of England are emptier than any deserted village. We are closer to our dead within the churches themselves.

The former All Saints Church, Wainfleet, demolished as unsafe in 1820

Chapter 10

Three Friends

CANON Overton, Rector of Epworth and church historian, pointed out the curious fact that Lincolnshire played a prominent part in the foundation of both the Society for the Promotion of the Gospel in Foreign Parts and the Church Missionary Society. Dr Willis, Dean of Lincoln, was associated with the beginning of the older body in 1701, and it was at a clerical meeting in Rauceby rectory in 1795 that a decision was taken which speeded the formation of what is known as C.M.S.

It could be added that a still younger society, now united with S.P.G., would not, humanly speaking, have survived its tragic beginning but for the work of three Lincolnshire incumbents. The Society was the Universities Mission to Central Africa and the incumbents were George William Tozer of Burgh le Marsh, Edward Steere of Little Steeping and Charles Argentine Alington of Muckton.

Tozer belonged to a family well known in South Devon, and had enough private income to contribute about £400 a year to the expense of the Mission during the time he was in Africa. After short curacies in London and North Kelsey he became Vicar of Burgh with Winthorpe in 1857. He was 28 years old. When Steere went to join him in 1858 he wrote, "am going to serve a man who shrinks from nothing and succeeds in everything".

The local school was in disorder. Tozer became master until the right man could be found. No one could be found to nurse a boy sick of a dangerous fever, so Tozer became a nurse. He ran a night school for a hundred and fifty youths of the neighbourhood. He installed organs in both churches. He shouted too much in church, but his popularity is attested by the fact that when he left Burgh two bricklayers, Richard Harrison and Thomas Sivil, went with him.

Steere came from a legal background and might have had a large practice at the bar but he chose otherwise. His first curacy was at Kerswell, near Tozer's old home. There he met Mary Brown. They were married a year after Steere came to Lincolnshire. He was ordained priest in Lincoln Cathedral on Trinity Sunday 1858. In those days examinations were not held until the Bishop gathered the candidates round him at Riseholme a few days before the ordination. It is said that some of the candidates looked down on Steere and that after the paper on Butler's *Analogy* one of them said, "Let me give you a tip. If you are ploughed by this morning's paper, get the edition with an introduction by a man called Steere, and if you know that you are sure to get through the next time." The author replied, "I have some acquaintance with that work."

Steere had to help Tozer and also act as curate for the absent rector of Skegness. Among the fishermen Steere soon gained the reputation of being 'a downright shirt sleeve man and a real Bible parson'. After eighteen months he became rector of Little Steeping. A rectory was built, the church was lighted and heated, school attendance trebled and a night school started. Little Steeping was being run on Burgh lines.

Charles Argentine Alington, who was born in 1828, belonged to a family that had been prominent in Lincolnshire for three hundred years. A kinsman was at Candlesby, which is only two miles from Burgh, and that may be how Tozer and Steere came to know him. He was ordained both deacon and priest in 1851 and became curate for a kinsman at Croxby. In 1853 he was presented to Muckton. In 1884 he went to Swinhope House and held the family living there. In the 1950s Muckton people still talked of how he brought home a black boy and how the stranger was killed by our English weather.

Bishop John Jackson of Lincoln was to be a strong supporter of the trio.

It has been said that the patron saint of U.M.C.A., one of the most Anglo-Catholic of societies, was the Presbyterian David Livingstone. It was Livingstone's rousing call to Cambridge in 1857 that lead to the formation of the Mission and he acted as its nursing father in its early days. On January 1st Charles Mackenzie was consecrated in Cape Town as Bishop to 'the tribes dwelling in the neighbourhood of Lake Nyassa and the river Shiré'. His small party made its way up the Zambesi. For over a year no news reached England. When it did it was to state that the Bishop and three of his party were dead. Tozer was consecrated as his successor in Westminster Abbey 2nd February 1863.

When Tozer was offered the bishopric, he asked if he might go over to Steere's rectory to talk the matter over. Before he arrived Steere, his wife and a lady friend were lunching. Steere said that he would advise his friend to accept. Mrs Steere looked up and said, "You had better go too, Edward, to take care of him". "Do you wish me to ?" he asked. She answered at once in the affirmative. "Very well then, I will," he said. Later he said that it did not seem right to advise his best friend to go and stay at home himself. Alington was of the same mind. So Steere could write, "We are going to transplant the same little circle of friends which was so pleasant here to our new scene on the Shiré". He thought the needs of the African population were incalculably greater than those of the English, and wanted to show that one's calling as a Christian priest is more than a comfortable home and easy-going quiet. Alington found an excuse to escape a Farewell meeting at Spilsby.

Perhaps the sacrifice of Mrs Steere is sometimes forgotten. The one or two years had become nearly six before her husband returned to England, and then the news was so bad he felt he must resign from Little Steeping. She bade him go. She meant to follow later, and twice came within sight of the steamer which was to take her overseas. Unfortunately she had a mental breakdown. She lived for a time at Hundleby, near Spilsby, and died in Lincoln Asylum in 1883. She was buried at Little Steeping.

A letter written to Bishop Jackson from the Cape shows that the party made a good impression there. Typically Alington dodged a Godspeed Party. An officer on the ship that carried them north stated there were a baker, mason, bricklayer and joiner in the party, so there were two craftsmen additional to the Burgh pair. "Neither the Bishop nor Alington are so strong in constitution as we would wish them to be. The Bishop suffers from a form of sciatica". Tozer's first episcopal act was a Confirmation on the ship. His second was to consecrate his predecessor's grave. On a lonely island he and Alington plunged through a jungle and after much searching found a pole with a piece of board as a cross-piece. After the prayers had been said they sang 'Nearer my God to thee'.

In his first year Tozer had decisions to take that met with the disapproval of Livingstone, the Home Committee and remaining members of Mackenzie's party. He soon decided that the Mission station was in an impossible place, and the party moved to the Morumbala Hills, two hundred miles nearer the coast, but fever followed them there. So Tozer decided to abandoned the Zambesi. The party then went to the Cape to decide on the best springboard from which to jump to Lake Nyassa. The Home Committee favoured Zululand, but Tozer was determined to do something for the east, even it if meant throwing up his commission as bishop and serving as a simple priest. He had decided on Zanzibar. He and Steere arrived there on 31st August 1864.

The second problem was that of associating working men with clergy. "The men who are with me are excellent fellows, but they feel the unreality of the situation as strongly as I do." The idea of setting up a little piece of English civilisation in the interior of Africa was perhaps a dream. A shoemaker who had accompanied Mackenzie and Tozer pointed out that "Africans do not wear shoes". But the failure was partly due to Tozer who carried English social distinctions with him and insisted on the mechanics dining at a separate table. Tradesmen have in fact shared in the life of the Mission and among them has been Joseph Oldridge of Barton on Humber. But when the pioneers left the Zambesi, Tom Sivil went home to talk about his efforts to teach Africans to speak English in a broad Lincolnshire accent.

Tozer's third difficulty concerned the dependents of the Mission. Moved by a generous impulse to join Livingstone in freeing slaves, the first party had collected nearly two hundred hangers on. Most were unwilling to go to the Morumbala Hills, but a few did. Tozer would take the orphan boys and use his own resources to help the females find a home. Waller, one of the first party, and Alington promised their maintenance would be no charge on Mission funds. "The people wish to be with us and we wish to have the work of protecting and teaching them," said Alington. However, he accepted Tozer's decision. Waller left the Mission and took the refugees south, and Livingstone claimed the boys.

Alington did not join Tozer and Steere in Zanzibar but returned to England. Tozer's letters give a glimpse of his friend down with fever, searching African villages for stolen goods, clearing the ground behind the Morumbala chapel for a garden, waiting for the orphan boys until Livingstone collected them, visiting a United Free Methodist Mission and approving of the choice of Zanzibar.

At Morumbala, Tozer had impatiently declared that a bishop does not simply do chores, but he and Steere found plenty in Zanzibar. The Sultan presented five slave boys to the Mission and British warships rescued more and brought them to the Mission. So Tozer and Steere became student teachers and house masters. He wrote to Mrs Jackson, "People of a sanguine temperament will be disappointed if they expect any immediate effect. It is an utter mistake that there is any way in which Africa can be won over to the faith that is in Jesus save that Royal one which His own blessed footsteps traced from the cradle to the cross."

In June 1865 Miss Tozer and other ladies came to help. Nine of the boys were baptised. One was called John after the Bishop of Lincoln. In May 1866 Tozer's hands were shaking so much that he could not write, and in September he left for England. Soon afterwards Alington returned to help Steere. Hitherto the difficulties of language had made it hard to do much beyond the walls of the Mission, but Steere's work on Swahili and two of the mainland dialects made it possible to start elsewhere.

In August 1867 Alington led a small party to the Usambara country. His account reads like pages from Ryder Haggard. Tramping across the red volcanic earth he came to the forbidden city of Vuga. After a night in a banana grove and much expenditure of gunpowder, the chief Kinweri made his presence felt. He sent the gift of a cow that was roasted whole at once, and he was represented on a hilltop outside the town by his eldest son. Alington presented the prince with a folding chair, and when the latter asked for medicine against evil spirits he spoke of prayer. The chief was willing to let the missionaries settle if the Sultan of Zanzibar consented, and although ill with fever Alington travelled to Zanzibar. He returned in January and fell in with a war party of Ziguas who were going to chastise the hill folk for daring to have rain when none had fallen in the lowlands. A message then reached him that Kimweri did not want the missionaries close to Vuga but that they might settle nearer the coast. So a station was set up at Magila and there Alington kept going throughout the wars that broke out on Kimweri's death.

Tozer returned to Zanzibar in July 1868. In the next month Steere left for England. He left his heart in Africa and busied himself seeing a Swahili gospel through the press. Towards the end of the year Alington, 'in a lamentable state', arrived from Magila to beg for reinforcements. Early in 1869 ill-health drove him back to England. There he twice became a rural dean, but otherwise there is little to distinguish him from the many priests who have laboured faithfully in small Lincolnshire parishes.

A week after his return from Magila, Tozer found he could not write. Then came a cholera outbreak. In April a cyclone wrecked the Mission House. In March 1872 Steere and Miss Tozer returned to Zanzibar. In May she wrote that the Bishop was broken down "sadly by all the trouble and nursing he has gone through". A holiday in the Seychelles did not work a cure. In January 1873 Tozer and his sister returned to England and there he resigned his post. He lived on for more than a quarter of a century, far from the land for which he would have given his life. He survived long enough to hear of the building of a cathedral on Likoma Island in Lake Nyassa. He outlived his two successors and both his friends. Although he did not consider himself worthy, Steere was consecrated bishop in Westminster Abbey on St Bartholomew's Day 1874.

When the Mission had been in effect without a bishop, a message had come from Magila, "Come over and help us". Fraser, Alington's successor, had died in 1870, but their work was not forgotten. Steere was the only priest remaining in the Mission, but on 8th October 1872 he commissioned four inexperienced subdeacons. Two were English and two were African. He said, "Brethren you are going on the noblest errand on which it is possible for men to go. You are sent to act as God's messengers, to publish his acts and explain his counsels. The more completely you forget yourselves and remember only Him, so much the better your work will be. God has looked with compassion on the sinful and miserable and sent you to tell him that He loves them'. That was the turning point of the work in Magila.

In 1873 a Hindu merchant gave Steere the site of the slave market in Zanzibar. Preaching soon began in a mud hut, and on Christmas Day the first stone of a permanent church was laid. It was opened exactly six years later. As a missionary wrote, "If any bishop has a claim to be represented in a stained glass window with a model of a cathedral in his hand, surely Bishop Steere has, for he was not only the architect but builder and clerk of works of the noble slave market church". He was still a 'shirt-sleeves parson'.

Steere refused to refer to that church as his cathedral. He insisted that a cathedral must be on the shore of Lake Nyassa. Early in his episcopate he made his walk to Nyassaland, and it is thought that the seeds of chronic ill health, which lasted to the end of his life, were sown in that walk in 1875. Nine slave caravans were encountered. In 1876 he made an expedition to find a spot where freed slaves might settle. He found it at Masasi. In 1877 he was back in England, but after a few day rest was active on Mission work. He was seen in a Lincolnshire wheelwright's shop 'finding out what was wrong with the wheels we make at Mbwene'.

In 1879 the first native deacon in the Mission was ordained, Steere's Swahili New Testament was printed in the native press, his translation of the Prayer Book completed, and another treck begun. A year later he encouraged pioneers to push out from Masasi to Lake Nyassa. In 1882 Steere paid his last visit to England, where his wife was very ill. In the same year he died in Zanzibar. He was 54. He is commemorated by a tablet in Little Steeping church and a window shows him ordaining an African.

Steere impressed people as a man of action who bent all his energies to one end. Intellectual and linguistic abilities were directed to the service of God in Africa. The depth of that commitment appears in his prayers. (I have had a copy of Bishop Steere's Prayer in my copy of *Sursum Corda* for seventy years.) As a young man he read six languages other than his own and studied Chinese for fun. In Africa he produced a Swahili handbook that has placed the Church in East Africa greatly in debt to him. As a Devon curate he lamented that he was far away from books, and he wrote other valued works beside the *Introduction to Butler's Analogy*. But he had small interest in scholarship for its own sake, although he could quickly tear the heart out of a book. The advice he gave was "Read a little and think a lot about it".

Some of his views were ahead of his time and when Bishop Wordsworth thought of founding a theological college in Lincoln he wrote to Steere for advice, but found his ideas too revolutionary. As for lay preaching he wrote, "It is a monstrous perversion to say that a man whose heart God has touched and to whom he has given great power to touch the hearts of others, shall in no case be allowed to use his power until he has learned to construe Greek".

Steere did not think he himself possessed the qualities needed by a missionary, but in his last sermon in England he spoke of the preaching of a life. "This power of quiet perseverance, this going about unacknowledged and unreceived, without the thankfulness of men, this going about doing good, this hiding oneself rather than coming forward to be seen, is the thing that had opened and does open the souls of men to God." He may not naturally have liked Africans but he did his utmost for them. "We love our fellow men not because they deserve it, but because we love God. The undeserved love of God is the basis of our hope. The giving of undeserved love is the perfection of our following God."

Tozer appears to be a strong-minded man who could not suffer fools gladly. He was really shy and awkward and needed friends. In 1868 he wrote to a friend that he would "dearly have loved to be at the anniversary, but I don't shine at such fêtes, especially since I have had the purple thrust on me, and seldom feel comfortable qua bishop anywhere". The years that followed his resignation from Zanzibar were years of growing loneliness and frustration. Twice he tried to resume episcopal duties – in Jamaica and Honduras. Each time it was only for a year. In May 1888 he became rector of South Ferriby in North Lincolnshire. The Parish Log Book makes us think that the glories of Burgh might be repeated. A choir wearing purple cassocks was introduced as also *Hymns Ancient and Modern*. The church was rebuilt and Tozer paid for the work on the chancel. On Low Sunday 1889 the Bishop of Lincoln performed the reconsecration, and in the remainder of the week there were great feasts, a Punch and Judy show and the release of a fire balloon. On 19th June Tozer retired. Once more his health had broken down.

His resignation was a renunciation. He left his horse and carriage and furniture to his successor. He spent some time in London, but most of this time was spent in Devon. One who knew him well wrote, "I have never known so striking detachment from the world. He seemed to form no new friendships and had no worldly belongings. It may be that in his years of frustration Tozer was learning the lesson all who work for God must learn. It is summed up in the words of the Baptist – "He must increase. I must decrease". Tozer planned his own funeral, so he probably planned his memorial which is in the churchyard of St David's, Exeter. On the top of the grave are a mitre and a pastoral staff. A cross bears the initials 'W.G.T.' and a footstone reads '1899'.

In 1874 the Burgh hairdresser Jabez Good carved an eagle lectern in gratitude for Tozer's ministry there, and in 1878 a Missionary College was founded in Burgh partly because there "Bishop Tozer animated his parishioners with missionary zeal and kindled the same in those about him". That college has long been closed. In the Marsh there is what was the Mission Church and School which he gave in 1867. The altar of the Missionary College is now in Burgh Church.

P.S. The man quoted above also wrote 'that Tozer rarely missed a daily service and gave large sums towards the restoration of the church'. He survived Alington by three weeks.

Jabez Good, the Burgh hairdresser,
used only a penknife to carve the
eagle lectern in the parish church

St Paul's College, Burgh

Chapter 11

Preacher and Sexton

SIR Edward Barkham, baronet, of Wainfleet All Saints, died in 1710. The baronetcy lapsed, and the Wainfleet estates passed to Edward Barkham. He was sometimes known as 'Edward Barkham of the East Indies' because he spent much of his manhood in that part of the world and in India. When he inherited he passed his days between Wainfleet, at the old manor house on the site of which the Angel now stands, Lincoln and London. When he died his body was brought from Lincoln to Wainfleet for burial in St Mary's church.

It was a costly funeral, for apart form the heavy leaden coffin, the total was over £327. That was thirty times what the vicar of a neighbouring parish received for looking after St Mary's parish. The sum of £80 was spent on gloves for mourners and £18 on mourning rings. Stops were made at Wragby, Horncastle and Spilsby for food. Carrying the corpse cost £26 15s. Servants received a shilling and the sexton 6s 8d. The account lies behind the following story-experiment. The sermon is based on sermons quoted in my PhD thesis 'Ecclesiastical and Religious Life in Lincolnshire 1640-1660'.

* * * * *

The pompous preacher mounted the pulpit and perched his spectacles on the end of his nose. He turned up the hour glass which would show when he had preached for an hour. Some of the congregation settled down to sleep.

"Brethren, when I think of the goodly concourse gathered here to-day I think of the host of Pharaoh's courtiers who accompanied Joseph and his brothers when their father's body was taken to its final resting place."

The sexton muttered, "This bunch stopped to guzzle food and swill wine every ten miles of the way. They gave old Pratty six shillings and eight pence and he'll clear up the mess when they've gone home."

"Brethren, I think of this generous man and I think of the centurion of whom the Jews said 'he loved our nation and built our synagogue.' He loved this house of God."

The sexton thought, "I wish he mended my leaking roof".

"Brethren, let us be like Joseph who had a tomb in his garden. Memento mori. One day we shall die, but we are like the pigeons in a church tower. The bells boom out and they fly away. The bells are silent and they return. Today you think of mortality. Tomorrow you will return to your richly laden tables, to the balls and games, to the chase and to running your estates and businesses".

The sexton grumbled, "It's old Pratty who clears up the mess the pigeons make."

"Brethren, I speak now of the Christian hope, the turning of the morning sonnets into marriage songs. For God has broken the teeth of the bloodhound death. The Prince of Peace has taken the clots and stone out of the grave, stuffed it with feathers and lined it with roses."

"A fat lot you know about clots and stones", grumbled old Pratt. "And I could tell him something about feathers. I bet he'd never plucked down feathers from a goose. Tonight when all this to-do is over I shall go home, sit by the fire, light my clay pipe, watch the brick warning on the hob, then wrap it up in flannel and climb the ladder to my feather bed. Amen to that."

Of course old Pratt was a grumbler. Compared with the total cost of that funeral, six shillings and eight pence was a kitten beside an elephant, but a very good week's wage.

In his will, Barkham made provision for St Mary's to have a full-time parson of its own. The bulk of his estate was left to Bethlem Hospital ('Bedlam') for the mentally ill. He had a special concern for those regarded as incurable. The hatchment or board on which his arms were painted to be carried at his funeral, as today medals might be carried on a cushion, is in the church.

Magdalen College. Wainfleet.

74

Chapter 12

Quincentenary

A SERMON preached by Canon J.E. Swaby MA PhD, former pupil of Magdalen College School, Wainfleet on 27th May 1984, on the occasion of the Quincentenary of the School building.

Psalm 27.13:1 *I believe that I shall see the goodness of the Lord in the land of the living.*

The trouble is not that old men forget but that they lapse into anecdotage. This old man will permit himself only one personal memory. Long ago when a sermon might seem as long as a giraffe's neck, my eyes might turn to a tablet on the wall in this church. It was in Latin and I could try out my knowledge of that language. It said that in the old All Saints' church was a tomb erected by William of Wainfleet to the memory of this father, Richard Patten. When the old church was broken up the tomb was broken too. The fragments are in Magdalen College chapel.

Let us go in imagination to that old churchyard on the Bank, find the site and picture the tomb. On the top there is a full length effigy of Richard Patten. His head rests on a cushion supported by miniature figures of William and his brother John. Below are two angels bearing shields. On one are the familiar lilies and lozenges. On the side are the words of my text in Latin: 'I believe that I shall see the goodness of the Lord in the land of the living'.

On that text I hang three things. The first is a brief account of the man who put those words on his father's tomb. The second is a thanksgiving for the many who have helped us see 'the goodness of the Lord in the land of the living'. The third is an attempt to show the relevance of those words for us today.

By now you may wonder how long this particular giraffe's neck is going to stretch. It will be a little longer than my usual sermon, but if you are bored the tablet is over there and you can test your own Latin.

In the 15th century it was not unusual for a son to be known by his place of origin rather than by his father's name. So William Patten became William of Wainfleet. We think of him as the local boy who made good by becoming the friend of King Henry VI, Bishop of Winchester and for a short time Lord Chancellor of England.

Like many bishops of the later Middle Ages, William was the custodian of large estates, and therefore was a power in the land. We picture him and his retinue moving, locust like, from estate to estate, eating up provisions as they went. Or we picture him at some stormy or anxious session around the King's Council table. But what distinguished him was his concern for education and for his native town. In those days monasteries had become unfashionable and what we call the 'New Learning' was gaining ground. As a result many wealthy men did not endow monasteries but schools.

Among these were William and his royal master. William's greatest monument is his college at Oxford, but he was also involved with Eton in its early days, and was remembered in the prayers offered in the chapel of King's College, Cambridge. His thoughts for his own town found practical expression when he helped to obtain for it a charter in 1458. Soil washed down from the Yorkshire coast was silting up the river mouth. The charter was a desperate attempt to save the little port. Twenty-six years later he built the school here. It is said that the building was modelled on a manor hose which he owned in Surrey.

As he believed that sound education is rooted in sound religion, the new edifice contained a chapel as well as a classroom and a master's lodgings. Its fortress like character reflects the turbulence of the times. For the Bishop lived in days when the War of the Roses cast a crimson shadow on the land. And it may not be inappropriate to apply to him words used in another disturbed age to describe Sir Robert Shirley, "Whose singular praise it was to have done the best things in the worst times and hoped them in the most calamitous."

In 1486 William of Wainfleet died and was buried beneath a great tomb in St Mary Magdalene's chapel in Winchester Cathedral. We should call him a great man, but let us not forget that the Christian means by greatness something more than a splendid sepulchre or an entry in the Dictionary of National Biography. True greatness requires readiness to spend oneself in the service of others and many humble folk have possessed that essential quality without being bishops or lord chancellors.

In the mists of five hundred years since 1484 are hidden many who would deserve commemoration if we only knew their names and deeds. And today there are many who still remember with affection and gratitude the work of those headmasters, the Reverend William Gerrish and Kenneth Gordon Spendlove, and of Florence Lucas and others who in our memories are indissolubly linked with the school in the time when the school gave more to the community than at any time in its history.

But this is a Wainfleet week and not only a Magdalen School one, so we must widen our thinking. I am tempted to dig into the past and mention William Reckitt, adventurous Quaker, Sarah Potter, a remarkable maid servant of the last century, and Mr Faulkner, vicar of St Mary's, whose lantern could be seen in St Michael's Lane on a winter's night bobbing up and down as he went to the mission church to pray for his people at the beginning of this century.

But each one of you will have known at least one person who has shown great devotion to duty or great care for others. We recall some self-sacrificing parent, some faithful Day or Sunday School teacher, some kind employer. Some conscientious workman, some true friend, or someone who has shown courage in suffering, going through the Vale of Misery and using it as a well. Thank God for such people for they are the salt of the earth without which society becomes rancid. They help us 'see the goodness of the Lord in the land of the living'.

So far I have spoken as if these words had reference only to life here and now, and that is what the man who wrote Psalm 27 thought about God's goodness. But Christians have read these words in the light of the resurrection of Jesus Christ. That is why William of Wainfleet put them on his father's tomb, and why I have used them at so many funerals. In that context the words say 'Enjoy life here to the full; value its sweetness; practise its goodness; but don't be short sighted. Try to see life in the light of God Eternal. Realise that nothing can separate us from Him'. There you have a sovereign remedy against pessimism.

During fifty years in the Christian ministry I have seen many despair for themselves and for the world This saddens me, but it does not surprise. A little experience of life is enough to discover the worm in the bud, the fly in the ointment. Our plans and dreams are very brittle.

There is some irony even in these celebrations. Many will rejoice that the Magdalen name and tradition live on in the new buildings on the Common, but some will also be sad that the old school was closed in the heyday of its powers. And there is the same irony in our lives. When we have at last gained a little vision, Death taps us on the shoulder and says, 'Move on please'.

Compared with our lives, the old school building seems very durable, yet even solid buildings which have stood for centuries will one day collapse like the sand castles before the incoming tide. Civilisations decline and fall.

I too would be gloomy if I could not see the light of the Resurrection, and hear the Christian gospel proclaiming that any goodness we know is but a foretaste of richer and fuller goodness and more abundant life beyond. It proclaims that no single good life, no single good deed, no one act of self sacrifice is ever finally lost or cast as rubbish to the void. It is caught up into the purpose of God. It becomes part of something that endures 'though hills shall melt and mountains fall into the sea'.

In that faith we can do the best things in the worst times and hope them in the most calamitous.

To God the Father, who shows his goodness here and hereafter;
To God the Son whose clear light is on our path;
To God the Holy Ghost through whom we may abound in hope;
To the One true God be all love and glory for time and for eternity.

The tomb of Richard Patten, father of William of Wainfleet, in the
old All Saints' Church. The miniature figure of William is on
the near corner and below is the angel and the text quoted

Chapter 13

Verses Old and New

Lincolnshire Memories

I've seen the youthful sun rise from the sea
And how its death throes set the Marsh ablaze.
I've seen the splendid rich days afterglow
Reflected on sand banks in Humber's flow.

I've shivered in a North Sea haar that froze,
Yet seen a cold sea mist break into smiles.
I've seen the molten slag on Scunthorpe banks
Light up the midnight sky for miles and miles.

I've seen the gentle friendly shire horse
The ploughman's sole companion on long days
When shining share cut furrows arrow straight
And squadrons of the gulls gave air displays.

I've heard the gentle swish of latticed sails
On mills now falling into slow decay.
Like mother ducks with ducklings in the wake
The chugging tugs pull barges Barton way.

I've heard the whirr of bygone binder blades,
The whistle of a shepherd to his dog,
The boom of bitterns in the feathered reeds,
The hoot of sirens in a river fog.

I've breathed the salty air upon the Flats
And plucked the 'samfer' from the muddy sand,
Touched bones of wrecks upon the shallow shore
Where men lost lives within a grasp of land.

Where once the pale sea lavender in bloom
And massed sea pinks did solitude adorn,
Where children's feet would slide upon the silt,
You see new acres of the ripened corn.

I've seen the boundless prairies of the Fens,
The serried ranks of tulip and of beet.
I've dreamed of days when there were duck decoys
And luscious cranberries for a London treat.

Beneath the cloudless dome of azure sky
Potato pickers cowered from the heat.
Sun bonnets hid a blank monotony.
The toil worn women were the Fen complete.

The rolling Wolds had lonely scattered farms,
Within the vales the village houses coil.
The shepherds and his flock traverse the heights
And barley grows upon the stony soil.

On windswept hills by battered lonely pines
The ghosts of ancient barrowed dead still march.
Through valleys run the chuckling chattering streams
And Welton Vale conceals a whalebone arch.

Within the Marsh the churches' clumps of trees
Broke up the vast expanse of pastoral green
Well spotted by the dots of Lincoln Reds.
The rooks hold synod and the herons preen.

Man's battled with the sea for centuries.
He might at times some precious acres gain,
Then through the battered banks and worn down hills
Would pour battalions of the greedy Main.

I've travelled on the arid draughty Heath
And felt wayfarers on the highway stark
Took heart when Dunstan Pillar's guiding light
Pierced through misleading robber dangered dark.

Beyond the Lincoln gap, below the Cliff,
Just where the water issues from the steep,
My father's forebears plied their village crafts
In forge and shop where snowflake shavings heap.

I've made my way along the limestone scarp
With sometime views across the eagred Trent,
the brackened waste and rhodadendroned woods
To Wesleyan worlds where Mother's youth was spent.

With clamorous summons or in winsome tones
The bells called 'Come to Church' and I might doze
When, after Cranmer's music, we'd arrive
At sermon time and parson's painful prose.

At times when shadowed by some soaring spire,
Amid the majesty of Minster shrine,
In towns and villages with 'two or three',
Life's turbid waters have been turned to wine.

In country cottages, on golden sands,
In crowded dusty adamantine streets,
In little towns which strangers think asleep,
Beneath appearances a strong heart beats.

My mind's a mansion filled with treasure trove:
This Turner of some well loved scene or place,
This music box of mem'ries magical,
The portrait of a well remembered face.

Wide Horizons

(Wainfleet the East Fen)

(1)

The wilderness of the Fen had disappeared.
Its face would sometimes scowl, but often smiled.
Some said that in the night the demons howled,
That phantom lights lured men to ghastly goals,
That shrieks of birds were cries of tortured souls.

The Deeps held half a hundred meres and more;
One numbered pools and runlets by the score.
The names are on an ancient map displayed:
The Sykes, Billwater, Cowgate and Matlade.

The Fen was not a useless stagnant bog,
Hostile to man but friendly to the frog.
The meres held stores of perch, pike, tench and bream
That would regale a modern angler's dream.

Eels pronged by stang made up a testy meal
The hungry child could not his joy conceal.
Peat turves were stacked beside the salter's door,
They help make salt from sleech come from the shore.
The cabin walls had woven willow strands.
Strong reeds were pliant in the thatcher's hands.
The lavish cranberry spread exuberant.
Fowl, berries, fish eked out a diet scant.
Part of the Fen dried out on summer days
And cattle from the vills went out to graze.

(2)

The slodger's life was solitary and hard.
It seemed at times no misery was barred.
Exposed to elements: sun, wind and rain
He shivered when fen fever came again.
He fished and fowled. What gentry called a sport
Was livelihood, his skill his last resort.
He owned a punt. He called it his old 'shout';
On dangerous waters made his way about.
He rarely smiled, his humour somewhat grim.
He cared for few and and few men cared for him,
But he was free, an independent man.
He kept no rules, no systematic plan.
The geese he reared made up his little store.
That was enough, he never asked for more.

(3)

The Fen is tamed but solitude remains,
Sparse homesteads scattered on the prairie plains.
A few small clumps of trees are sometimes seen,
They mark the site where duck decoys have been.
The drained fen roads are bleak and blank and bare.
The traveller has little change of fare.
A distant tractor in a haze of heat,
A lorry laden to the top with beet
Perhaps are all that meet the searching eye
Beneath the dome of widely spreading sky,
But laughter's there within the new turned earth,
Rejoicing in the promise of new birth.
There's beauty in the clouds so lightly curled,
In ones that sail like ships with flags unfurled
Or sable cloud that's edged with silver gleams.
There's pageantry beyond the poet's dreams.
Forget the boundless dull monotony,
See how the sunsets die exquisitely.
The Artist's colours are both rich and bold,
The green and crimson mixed with purest gold.

Louth Park Abbey

A grey and lichened stretch of wasted wall
Betrays the spot where rose the abbey tall.
Once graceful lines in peaceful beauty flowed
Where now in later spring the gorse bush glowed.
The ragwort and the pimpernel abound
On what to men of old was holy ground.
Where once cowled monks came down the dorter stairs
In chilly dawn to chant the Mattins prayers
The linnet sings upon a willow bough
And plainsong is the windswept reed bed's sough.
And where the cattle shelter from the sun
Lay brothers entered in their labour done
Behind ox plough or carting sheaves of corn.
Their clothing caked, their faces weather worn.
The fleeces shorn from sheep by their skilled hands
Were borne across the sea to foreign lands.

A modern long haired youth jean-clad youth once strode
Across this ancient site of monks' abode.
A strange contraption clamped upon his head
Gave deep impression that he walked while dead.
Tape driven waves of throbbing mounting sound
Hurled in the ears had left his senses drowned.
His background was our arid cultural waste
Whose bread of life is crisps with onion paste,
Salvation's Cup a coca-cola tin
Discarded anywhere but in a bin.
His mother worshipped in a superstore:
Large Flush costs fifty pence and nothing more.
His father said the bishops were all fools,
But muttered prayers when filling in the pools.
Their visions bright were violence and lust
Which pundits call 'A Television Must'.
His mother's heaven an Aston Martin car,
His father's Avalon a round in par.
Their gospel was a tabloid's daily rant,
Some sordid tale spiced with a lot of cant.
A deadly venom poisons human lives
Where savants snigger and where Mammon thrives.

Why came this youth into this place apart?
Was there a trackless desert in his heart?
Was this an idle hour to spend in bale
Or was he blindly groping for the Grail?

A silent wraith bent low his tonsured head
'Bless souls in Paradise and living dead.'

Old St Peter's

Such is the name of what remains of the Saxon church at Barton on Humber. The chancel arch survives but not the chancel. A door separates old Saxon and later Gothic. The day of St Peter in Chains is 1st August or Lammas Day.

Here is no afterthought,
Codicil to Gothic.
Here grizzled grandsire
Content by fireside
Let Gothic puff and prate.
Rock like solidity,
Austere simplicity,
Music of ancient song
Borne on the wings of time,
Relic of Saxondom.

Lammastide once again.
Through the still sleeping streets
Come a few worshippers.
I had an insight then.
Short as a lightning strike,
Torn from the veil of time.

There stood a tonsured priest,
Vested in coarsest stuff,
Voice gruff and tremulous.
In the old chancel space
Serfs were in tower-nave.
Clothes reeked of soil and beasts.
Latin was double dutch,
But at Hic Corpus est
All on the rushes knelt.
Though we used different rites
His prayers and mine were fused.
Ancient and modern met.
Christ opens times-shut doors,
In Him our paths converged.

Uffington Churchyard

In Uffington St Michael's spire
 In stately grace soars over all.
The smaller spires of pink and white
 Burst on the chestnuts lordly tall.
As leaves unfurl on summer days
The limes are lyrical with praise.

In Uffington throughout the year
 The churchyard yews straight soldiers stand
Great grenadiers in tunics green,
 A goodly and a gallant band,
Two ranks that through the ages bring
Fit honour guard for Christ the King.

In Uffington in early year
 The snowdrops droop in gentle grace
Like maiden shy who fain would hide
 The beauty of a stainless face.
White burning lights on earth bound clod,
The pure in heart who see their God.

At Uffington the aconites
 Are golden coins in largesse thrown
From fiery chariots of the sun,
 In wild profusion richly strewn,
The aureate pieces tribute pay
To Christ who walks our common way.

In Uffington on damp dark days
 There swells a flood of pale primrose,
A promise of the coming spring
 The yellow splendour softly glows.
So is Christ raised, the promise true
Of risen life for me and you.

In Uffington at Easter feast
   Beside the path gleam daffodils
That smile to greet the risen Lord.
   Their golden glory overspills
In waving, joyful, dancing tides
That ebb and flow for Easter brides.

In Uffington you seek in vain
   For formal cemeterial plan
Of chill math'matic symmetry
   Devised by bureaucratic man.
The trees and flowers, the bees and birds
Are poetry beyond all words.

In Uffington man's dust and ash
   Are dense within the hallowed ground,
But on another brighter shore
   The trumpet calls to life resound.
Lord grant all music, beauty, peace
Where darkness, discord, dolours cease.

A New Heaven and a New Earth

(Tallington)

Romans 8.20-1 *The creation itself shall be set free*

Her eyes
See not the odourous filth of bats
As birdsong floats through open doors,
Accompaniment for Eucharist.

She sees
Through clear glass window lights
The breeze swayed leaves upon the trees
Reflecting gleams of morning sun.

Her voice
With heart uplifted to the Lord
Is joined in threefold holy song
Trisagion of angel hosts.

She feels
An unheard wave of worship surge.
The speechless world outside the church
Is bursting into songs of praise.

Silent
The fleecy clouds in deep blue sky,
The hips and haws in tangled hedge,
The candle flames on chestnut trees.

And dumb
The waddling duck so comical,
The darting fish, the grazing sheep.
Yet all proclaim the King of Kings.

The Lord
Takes things of earth to consecrate;
The bread that's made from soil born wheat,
The wine that oozes from the sun kissed grape.

Transformed
Creation in mute bondage held
Will shout its song of liberty,
Rejoicing with the sons of God.

The Cricket Match

Our village had a cricket team,
    Its colours blue and red.
It plays close by the Bread and Milk
    And near the railway shed.

Our captain is a little old,
    More than a little fat;
He cannot bend to pick up balls,
    He cannot see to bat.

He played at some far distant time
    For Rutland's Second side.
He still does lots of gardening
    And bowls a deadly wide.

The vicar is a timid man
    And somewhat out of date.
He leaves to polish sermons up
    If we play rather late.

The butcher's a practitioner
    Of fancy cut and chop.
He has a preference in the field.
    He likes to play long stop.

The gentle Godfrey bowls high lobs;
    He tosses them so high
That Perks, the postman, once declared
    'That touched the bloomin' sky'.

Our keeper is long past his best,
    'He stoppeth one of three'.
We can't omit him from the side.
    His wife provides the tea.

Our umpire is of value great,
    For if some foreign bat
Gets settled in and runs come fast,
    We simply shout 'How's that'.

Our annual game with Uffingham
    Is highlight of the year,
They prime themselves with lemonade,
    We brace ourselves with beer.

We took the field with three men short.
    The vicar, sad to say,
Had lost himself in his big books
    And quite forgot the day.

The postman, coming a few miles
    Upon his sit and beg
Acquired a puncture in the lane.
    He has a gammy leg.

When someone asked why he was late,
    Young Smithson made reply
'My Missus kept me in the house
    Until my shirt was dry'.

When Uffingham went in to bat
    We started rather well.
A dozen runs were on the board
    When their fourth wicket fell.

All this was due to blacksmith's scowl
    And to his semi throws.
He hit Smith in his wide midrift
    And Johnson on the nose.

Jim Gibson gave a dolly catch
    The barrage to evade,
It fell in Watson's trousers
    Which were a trifle frayed.

Their skipper took one on the head,
    We gave a mighty shout,
Our keeper took his season's catch,
    Our umpire said 'That's out'.

The man looked up in dazed surprise,
    His language was not good.
Our joiner umpire then declared
    'I know the sound of wood'.

When Godfrey started with his lobs
    Old Perks went for a nip.
He keeps a bottle near at hand
    When fielding in the dip.

One hit a mighty towering ball
    To captain in the deep.
He slipped upon some excrement,
    Collided with a sheep.

In wild pursuit of needed runs
    Two men crashed head to head.
We were concerned to pick them up
    And tuck them up in bed.

Their fifty eight was quite a lot
    For our small village team.
We sought to keep our spirits up
    With captain's Bristol Cream.

Our worry was a needless thing;
    We soon obtained the score.
Ten minutes time was quite enough
    We had to take no more.

The blacksmith gave a hefty slog;
    A goods train rattled by.
The ball fell in an open truck
    That carried on to Rye.

Our batsmen ran and ran and ran
    'til we reached fifty nine
Our umpire said to all protests
    'There is no boundary line'.

And Uffingham grew rather cross
    And some began to brawl,
And not a single one of them
    Had sense to call 'lost ball'.

With all the exercise the pair
    Were very weak and pale.
We took them to the Bread and Milk
    For Ruddles Rutland Ale.

For cricket I am now too old.
    I dream of railway trucks.
And just to show I keep in touch
    I'm rearing lots of ducks.

Janna

The day you walked into our house
    You stepped into our hearts,
A lady gentle in your ways,
    Endowed with courtly parts.

A Cavalier from line of Kings,
    With tiny winning face
You deigned to claim us as your own
    With such a lovely grace.

You loved it when we spoke to you
    In soft caressing tone,
Your eyes would shine with pure delight
    To say 'I'm yours alone'.

When you went deaf then other ways
    Must human voice replace.
We learned to speak to you by signs
    And you could read a face.

When we had been away from you,
    You'd sense when we neared home,
And at the door your tail would wag
    Just like a metronome.

When mistress came home from the church
    You gave her special cheer;
As she bent down to pat your head
    You'd lick her on the ear.

To guests who came into the house
    A welcome you'd extend,
As if in doggy way you said
    'I'm glad you called, my friend'.

'Descended from a line of Kings',
    'A dainty little dog',
Yet when your mistress minced your meat
    You were a little hog.

And then we'd see your rounded tum
    And try hard to be stern,
But we were putty in your paws
    When you put on your turn.

Upon your walks along Love's Lane
    You'd stop to take delight
In 'doggy news', but run at speed
    Ere we went out sight.

You always knew just when to turn
    And take the homeward track.
You'd dash in for a bowl of tea
    The moment we were back.

A wise old lady said to us
    'Don't give a dog your heart
Or else a sword will pierce your own
    When you and it must part.'

We paid no heed, we gave you love
    And you gave joy to us
In many years of happiness.
    You were an alpha plus.

When you were ill you looked to us,
    That was not very odd
For in your little canine mind
    We humans were your god.

Within the garden which you loved
    Your little body lies
Close to another of your friends,
    Our Sara's Ani wise.

You were at once a humble serf
    And yet Your Majesty,
But most of all you ever were
    One of the family.

A photo' seems to sum it up.
    Upon a large settee
You nestle close to Mary's side
    With Rob, Fiona, me.

Swaledale

Below our eyrie on the wind swept moor
The tourists' cars are only match box toys
Drawn by a thread of dusty grey that weaves
Beside the brown and silver of the Swale.
The campers on the tree fringed meadow field.
Are midgets in a mini-circus troupe.
A pair of hikers, pack humped, scanning maps,
Are insects crawling slowly o'er great stones,
Although for them this long planned walk will be
The great adventure of a week so full
Of memories of flowers that clothe the grass
More richly than the robes of Solomon,
Of gentleness within these towering hills
As if some giant had stooped down to smile
His welcome, and of cropping casual sheep.

As we take out our sandwiches and flask
One of the Swaledale breed invites herself
To be spectator of our human ways,
(So far removed from thrusting Goathland ewes
That rear and paw your chest, demanding food),
She stares and weighs us up and then departs
Into the miles of heathered wilderness,
Indifferent to these things from outer space.

There is much debris left by men who mined
For lead within these hills for centuries.
We see a ghostly packhorse train
With loads of lead for Fountains Abbey roofs.
And now from up the dale to Grinton church
Another group moves slowly on Corpse Way.
Those ghost men from the lonely farms would walk
In quiet tribute to some time worn friend
Whose dogs would miss his long deliberate stride,
Whose sheep would miss his quiet Yorkshire voice.

The silence of hills this summer day
Is that of life if we have eyes to see,
Can tune our ears to different frequencies
From that of offices and crowded streets.
But when the autumn leaves have faded fast
And winter tightly grips a snow bound dale,
A silence fearful and yet beautiful
Imprisons both the farmer and his beasts.
The frozen hands dig deep for buried sheep
Or break the ice upon the sleeping streams.
And by the fire the children kept from school
See fancied pictures in the burning coals.
This enforced gelid silence isolates.

Start of the Third Millennium

What do we celebrate? Mere change of date
Will not itself bring in a Golden Age
When wars will be no more and children walk
Unharmed along our lanes and city streets.
The tooth that aches before the midnight hour
Will still give pain when New Year's corks have
popped.

Will it be more than jamboree,
A New Year's party on gigantic scale,
Or shall we pause awhile, for once forget
The rat race and the advertiser's rant,
The politicians prattle and the media slant?
Perhaps we'll stop and ask what A D means,
Years of our Lord, the years of Jesus Christ.

Two thousand years ago or thereabouts,
The Light of Lights shone in a stable mean
When God Incarnate came as truly man
To share our lot, to work with toil worn hands,
To die the victim of our human hate.
Yet, risen, is alive for evermore,
The Lord of loyal hearts and rightful king
Of all the world.

That light the darkness has not overcome.
The light still shines in little mud walled shrines
Or tabernacles in the distant dales,
Beneath great towers that rise in majesty
Or soaring spires that upward lift the heart.

Throughout the world Christ's followers gave gone,
Through darkest forest depths and barren wastes,
By mountain paths and to the lonely isles
To crowded city streets and stinking slums.
In name of Christ they've borne aloft a torch.
Lit from his light, it sometimes flickers low
Then mounts aloft a radiant flame.

The light of freedom shone upon the slave;
The light of hope for children in deep mines;
The light of knowledge in the Christian schools;
In pioneering work in hospitals.

In history's pages some wrote names in gold,
But most of all a mighty multitude
Of quiet humble folk who sought no fame,
Lit candles in their homes and neighbourhood.

Gimcrackery of domes is not the way
To thank the Lord while thousands elsewhere starve,
Let's have our fun, there's room enough for that.
But let's lift up our hearts in gratitude.
Lord open our blind eyes that we may see.

Chapter 14

Forty-Two Years

THIS is not a story of my life. I have written about that elsewhere for my daughter and my grandchildren. Family has always meant much to me. I had a happy childhood and am grateful for 44 wonderful years of marriage. I am proud of my daughter and her children. I prefer, however, to give thanks for happy memories quietly.

I had not intended to say much about my 42 successive years of ministry in the diocese and county of Lincoln, but have come to realise that I must say something more in fairness to the people I have known.

My parents went to the Wainfleet Wesleyan chapel in the evening. My brother and I went to the chapel Sunday School in the afternoon and later to chapel in the morning. I retain my admiration for the two railwaymen who gave up their afternoons to teach in the Sunday School. Then one Sunday Father took us boys to see his parents in Scampton. His two unmarried sisters and their young men went in the evening to Aisthorpe church. It is possible that father wanted to talk to his parents without us listening. After that we asked if we might go to church. It is probable that sermons there were shorter. Permission was given and in time we were confirmed by Bishop Swayne. Our sisters took the same path and became regular worshippers.

It was the goodness of my Mother and the remark of my music teacher, Florence Wilson, that made me think of ordination. She stopped the lesson to suggest that I should be a teacher or a priest.

Then came what some would call coincidences but which I see as something more. I had gone as far as the Wainfleet school could take me and it was a matter of boarding school. My father wrote to both Spalding and Louth Grammar Schools. He set out to go to Spalding but on the way remembered something in the Louth headmaster's letter that had impressed him. He turned round and I went to Louth, and gained two university scholarships.

Then came the second event. A laymen named Edmund Stephens was staying in Wainfleet assisting the priest doing locum duty. He came into our shop and talked with Mother. He told her that he was to be ordained and go as a curate to Louth. Moreover his brother-in-law had links with a Durham college. To him I owe a great debt. In term time I would go with him to the Union Workhouse chapel and it was there as a schoolboy that I preached my first sermon. Then we went on to Welton le Wold for Evensong and I read a lesson. It was he who suggested to the rector that I could be a possible future curate. So I went to Louth for a three years curacy and stayed seven.

I select one Louth memory for mention. It is both sad and unforgettable. I also discovered later there were links with my past of which I was unaware. A choirboy named Geoffrey Baggaley was dying of Hodgkinson's disease. I visited him almost every day. One day after I had given him Communion, he produced a splendid red stole which he had bought with his own money. I think he knew the end was near. He said that he had meant to give it to me at Christmas, but he wished to give it to me now, I buried him before Christmas. I kept in touch with his parents. His mother Ida lived to the age of 104. Only after her death did I see a photograph of the descendants of the centenarian Mrs Waite of Croft. She later moved to Wainfleet to be near her son Fred. He was Ida's uncle. Once I went back from Louth to Wainfleet All Saints' to take the wedding of Ida's cousin Jack. Still was I unaware of the link. Fred's widow had obtained permission for me to officiate. The best man let Jack in on the secret, but his bride Kathleen did not know. As a girl she had come to our Christmas parties and there was a look of delighted surprise as she saw me standing at the chancel step.

Mrs Sharpe was an unobtrusive member of the Scunthorpe St John's congregation. She came regularly to Evensong and sat with a kneeler in the small of her back; she had strained it in caring for others. Her husband had sleeping sickness. He was ill for years. When I saw him he was always lying on a couch. How she got him to the outside toilet I never asked. When he died she had small respite before she had to care for her aged father. One day I looked in. She was worried because she had some shopping to do. I offered to stay with her father while she did it. In her absence he died. On her return she exclaimed 'Thank God'. She did not mean that life would be easier for herself. She meant that she had been given strength to care for him to the end. The 'down town' population had many like that.

*The author with his wife Mary on the occasion
of the christening of their daughter Sara
at Mablethorpe in September 1959.*

Interior of Theddlethorpe All Saints

Memories of Mablethorpe said nothing about the two Theddlethorpe parishes which must not be passed over although there was only one person to every ten acres of land. The heating system of All Saints' church had not functioned for many years and services were held in the vicarage. We decided to bring the church back into use. Women cleaned and even scrubbed the mould off the nave pillars. Men wired the belfry to keep out pigeons and carted away loads of pigeon dirt. A great stack sheet covered the screen and we were kept warm in the chancel by oil stoves which Henry Shelbourn tended.

The wall and roof of the south aisle were about to collapse. With the help of St Helen's and aid from Canada and elsewhere we saved them. Two things are noteworthy. Some green sandstone had to be replaced. Mr Shelbourn asked if he might have some of the decayed stone to put down in his crew yard. Hit by a hammer it collapsed like a sand castle. Then joiners of Mawers of Louth so blended old and new roof timbers that visitors could not tell where one lot ended and the other began. The masons dug under the south wall yard by yard and poured concrete into the foundations. Again there was little to see.

It was due to Mr Shelbourn's enthusiasm that I took the large W.E.A. classes on which *The Marshmen* is based.

One cannot omit Jacob Rooney from the St Helen's story. He was the last incumbent of Tallington alone. Later I was to hold that benefice as part of the Uffington Group. After he contracted Parkinson's disease he and his wife moved to Trusthorpe to be near friends. I met Mrs Rooney in Mablethorpe Library. She asked me to call but the rector of Trusthorpe did not welcome intrusion. However she wrote to the Archdeacon to ask if he could find work for Jacob. He asked me as Rural Dean to see what I could do. At that time I had Evensong at St Helen's on Sunday afternoon. I talked generally about his helping there. I got up to go but at the door I turned round. What made me do it I do not know. I said, "We'll start next Sunday". If I had not done so he might never have started. He insisted on going in his electric chair. Mrs Rooney followed slowly and anxiously in a taxi behind. I brought up the rear ready for emergencies. People were most helpful and gradually he took more and more of the service from the chair. After I left I heard about a festival when there should have been a Communion Service. The old priest helping in the vacancy had forgotten to turn up. When Rooney heard this he said, "You shall have it", and he celebrated. Later the couple moved to Kirkby on Bain. On his death his widow gave his private Communion set to Bill Annakin who had been with me at Barton.

A story about Theddlethorpe is worth recording. Down a lane that ended on the river bank were a few houses. At one time there had been a family with 12 children, and 16 in the Baddley household. Farther on was a house where 20 children had been born. Soon after my arrival I went, late at night, to see the mother of the score. The doctor said that she would not last the night. He thought that she was unconscious. She heard him and that was the stimulus she needed. She would show him. She was still alive when I left the area.

One Sunday there was a great blizzard. I was due at Theddlethorpe three times. When I returned from the second trip loose telephone wires tangled with the under part of the car. I could not get out the third time nor send a message. Later it was good to know that they had performed a D.I.Y. act. For four days we had no electricity or 'phones and only such water as was in the tank. The end of my deprivation was comical. I went into a shop and asked for a dozen candles, only to be told that I might have one. When I explained that I wanted them for house-bound people, I got the packet. On reaching home I found that in my absence services had been restored. So yellowing and twisted candles cluttered up a cupboard for years. On that stormy Sunday a faithful few walked through knee deep snow to the Mablethorpe church for Evensong. Fortunately the church was heated by gas and when electricity was installed for lighting the old gas pipes had been left in place. So we carried on by the flickering light of gas jets. At St Helen's the storm solved one problem. A churchyard tree was overhanging telephone wires and to deal with it would have been costly, but as the wires were down it was dealt with swiftly.

For two reasons I must give greater space to Barton on Humber. The first is that it was the high point of my wife Mary's contribution to church music. I was then rural dean of Yarborough with more than thirty parishes. In January 1969 a televised service was held in St Mary's to celebrate the bringing of Christianity by St Chad to North Lincolnshire 1300 years earlier. Dr Coggan, Archbishop of York was the preacher. Mary had trained a choir for seventy drawn from all but one of the choirs of the deanery. There was a rehearsal on the evening before the transmission. At the last moment the choir asked Mary to conduct. Soon the Anglia TV Religious Director came out of the commandeered vestry to ask that Mrs Swaby might stand elsewhere as her arm kept appearing in the picture. I said that she did not mind where she stood, but I hoped that our daughter watching at her boarding school would get one good view of her mother. So Mary sat with the choir. Soon the Director was back again. The singing was so good the choir need

The televised service in St Mary's, Barton on Humber
January 1969 (Photos: David Lee)

L-R: Rev John Swaby, the Archbishop of York, Dr Coggan,
and the Bishop of Grimsby, Rt Rev G.F. Colin

*The author with his wife Mary who trained the
Yarborough deanery choir for the televised service
(Photo: David Lee)*

remain no longer. Then his secretary came to say that Sara would get a good view. Mrs Coggan was watching the transmission at home. Naturally the Archbishop made several references to St Chad. That was the name of their dog. And every time the dog heard his master's voice the dog responded. At last he went to lie in the doorway to wait for the Archbishop's return. She told Mary this when we met her later in the year.

The other thing that should be related is the breaking down of denominational barriers. There was a long history of intolerance in Barton. A few weeks after my arrival the Salvation Army asked me to chair their Christmas Carol Service. When I got back home I told Mary "These people do enjoy their religion". The next day a well disposed driver stopped his lorry to grin and say, "You have put your foot in it". Among others well disposed was the remarkable carver Phil Pape whose deep cut lettering may be seen on many a plaque in Lincoln. He lived at Tyrwhitt Hall. The original mediaeval timber-frame hall had become a barn. He restored it and its gallery. There he gave concerts. He had his own choir. By the time I arrived in Barton all the men had left the church choir. It was near Christmas Eve and boys could not be expected to turn out for the Midnight Service. Phil came to see me. Many of his choir were Methodists, well aware that in those days they could not receive Communion. Yet they practised Merbecke and sang it well.

My arrival coincided with that of a new Methodist minister, Ray Blackburn, a new Congregational minister and Salvation Army officer. Soon we had a new Roman Catholic priest. We knew what we wanted. Soon we were meeting every Monday morning for prayers. Criticism came. I invited Ray to preach at a weekday Lent service. A churchwarden resigned on grounds of conscience. Then the Methodists broke a promise to Ray to invite him to stay an extra year on the excuse that he planned to close the chapel and take them all to church. No wonder Mother said 'Thank God' when I said that I chose the Church of England. In her young days chapel and circuit officers had even more power over ministers. Her local preacher father used to say, "First year idolise; second criticise; third year scandalise". The stay was then three years. In the Church of England we may talk of summering and wintering a man before we trust him.

We were not fully aware of the big step we were taking. We just got on with the job. Ray and I took part in the dedication of a new Salvation Army citadel. United Good Friday services were started. When the Congregational church was without a minister and it was their turn for the Armistice Sunday service they were happy for me to fill the gap. Ministers changed but co-operation went on. Then we started mid-week Lent services in each place of worship in turn for a service typical of that place. All were crowded.

What was happening was seen in the televised service. Representatives of four other places of worship were there with our own people and those of the Deanery, the Roman Catholic priest, the Methodist and Congregational ministers and the Salvation Army officer were in the chancel with the Deanery Clergy and stood on the chancel step by the Bishop of Grimsby and some Deanery clergy as he read the special Litany for the occasion. Douglas Ross, headmaster of the C. of E. Primary School, and his staff were strong supporters of these forward moves. I went into the school twice a week and then one day the staff, not all of whom were Anglicans, asked if I could give them some instruction. I did this while Mr Ross took the whole school in singing. When the Bishop of Lincoln came for the celebration of the school's centenary I asked that the Methodist and Baptist teachers should be allowed to receive Communion. Permission was gladly given. Today one would not need to ask.

The Holy Spirit is ever active although it is often only in retrospect that we know that we have been His instruments. It was only just before we left Barton that I realised that it was more than chance that the original five came together to break down barriers.

My last five years in the diocese of Lincoln were with the Uffington Group. I would tease Mary by saying that the wardens of the parishes chose me because they were really choosing an organist. She played in all three churches. One of the great events of those years was a Country Life Festival. Mary and I set the ball rolling, but it was the real communal effort of a village at its best. It was in Uffington that I saw my great great grandfather's long cased clock. Inside was the name 'John Swaby'. He gave it to his daughter when she married and Mrs Carter of Uffington was one of her descendants. My last service was on Easter Low Sunday 1976. On Good Friday I had taken the Good Friday Three Hours Service in Lincoln Cathedral.

I have had good curates and wardens. Of curates I recall Arthur Muxlow and Jeffrey Frogatt at Barton and Bill Annakin and Sam Radford at Barton. For most of the time Cyril Dobson and Haydn Williams were the Scunthorpe wardens. Bishop Greaves called us 'The Boys'. At Theddlethorpe All Saints I was lucky to have Henry Shelbourn and Ted Baddley, and at St Helen's Jack Robinson and John Smith. The latter had just retired after fifty years service.

On the occasion of the author's farewell at Uffington in 1976. L-R: Robin Lowe, Sara Swaby, Canon John Swaby, Mrs Mary Swaby and 'Nobby' Noble

On the 50th anniversary of the author's ordination, on 26th February 1984 at Barnack. L-R: Canon C. Mayhew, Rev Bill Annakin, Monsigneur Mark Swaby, Sara Swaby, Canon David Rutter, Mrs Mary Swaby, Mr Crowson, Canon Dr John Swaby, Rev Grahame Smith and Canon J.W. Parker

Because the two large churches in Barton were sometimes regarded as being separate parishes there were four wardens. In the first part of my time there the wardens were 'the beloved physician' George Birtwhistle, Hugh Varah, Jack Taylor and Jack Kitching. At the time of the televised service they were Dr Birtwhistle, Kenneth Cox, John Townsend and Clifford Smith, and admirably they performed. I was fortunate too in the Uffington Group. At Uffington there were Robin Lowe and 'Nobby' Noble; at Barholm 'Jof' Flint and Bob Baldwin; and at Tallington Mr Thomas and Alan Thurlby. Alan still goes strongly.

The last 26 years have been spent in the diocese of Peterborough, but I have always maintained links with Lincoln and in September 2002 I had the joy of attending the service there and sitting in my old stall of Farrendon. In the same month I and Sara had three days in North Yorkshire walking the tracks where Mary and I used to walk.

For the first eight years of retirement we were at Southorpe in the parish of Barnack, and I rejoiced to have Lincolnshire still as part of my address. It was good to work with Canon Mayhew and it was in Barnack that the 50th anniversary of my ordination was kept. It was quite a Lincolnshire occasion. David Rutter, Precentor of Lincoln cathedral preached. When we visited Lincoln, Mary played duets with him. Canon J.W. Parker, who had been made a deacon when I was ordained a priest, proposed the toast. He mentioned the time when we met unexpectedly when walking in the Lake District. Sara was beginning to have serious back trouble and could walk no farther, but happily his car was near. Bill Annakin took part in the service as did my cousin Monsigneur Mark Swaby who came specially from London. (When Mark died I took part in his Requiem Mass.) There was a contingent from Barton, and Grahame Smith, my successor at Uffington, had cancelled morning services so that people from that group were well represented.

For the next 18 years I helped out in Empingham and kept things going during three vacancies. Good friends there will understand, however, that this is a chapter about 42 years in the Lincoln diocese and it would be out of place to say more. I should, however, like to pay tribute to Bishop Paul Burrough, Norman Rom and Archdeacon Fernyhough and John Heffer. With them I would like to associate David Monk and John Partridge who recently retired after long service. Nor must I omit Stanley Hoar. I have known him and Nancy since 1956. Until recently he gave real service to Empingham church that deserves recognition.

Conclusion

HAVING with some hesitation entered into some details of my Lincoln ministry, a few generalisations may be in place.

I have known great joy and great sorrow. A priest or minister not only has to lead worship but also carry people on his heart. What helped me to enter into tragedies was the fact that even before ordination I believed that when human hearts are breaking there is aching in the heart of God.

There have been many failures. There are ink and tear stained pages that I should like to rewrite but cannot. There are also delightful surprises. In retrospect even disappointments can be seen as blessings for oneself or for others.

I have come to value greatly the rank and file of worshippers. Many 'trace the rainbow through the rain'. They do not sound trumpets or throw their weight about, but green is the memory of them.

The first 37 years of ministry saw little relaxation. Mablethorpe was meant to be a little easing up but then the flood came. Sometimes I took six services on a Sunday as well as a Sunday School class. But as Mother said, "Better to wear out than rust out".

Three churches in which I once officiated have been closed. I have written at some length about Scunthorpe Parish Church. After all we tried to do in Theddlethorpe All Saints it is sad to read in a recently published book that there are more birds inside the building than outside. At Barton on Humber we spent a very large sum restoring St Peter's Saxon tower, but then found it impossible to maintain two large churches so close together and still pay a large quota to the diocese. So St Peter's was left to the mercy of the archaeologists.

I was sad and sore about all three, but a church with a small c is not the Church with a large capital letter. The one consists of stone and mortar, the other of people. Blow up all the churches in Lincolnshire and the Church will go on even if its members meet in houses, barns or schools.

In the chancel of St Mary's church in Barton on Humber there is a monument to Jane Shipsea who died in 1626. She died in childbirth aged 22. Her husband was rector of a nearby village, but they lived in Barton. After a short description in Latin of her virtues we read "such walles do make God's house, true living stones Ingraven as we by God". John is telling us that his wife and people like her were living stones in God's spiritual temple which is the Church. It is spiritually disastrous to worship stone and mortar and not God. 'Where two or three are gathered together in my name there am I in the midst of them.'

One of the sadnesses of old age is to find that one outlives old friends. Yet one discovers the meaning of the Communion of Saints. In the Bible 'saints' refers to all Christians. "One family we dwell in Him, One church above beneath". Bishop King of Lincoln used to say that on earth we make friends and in heaven we can enjoy them.

I began with tales. The one which follows may not be true but it makes a point. The rector was offered a bottle of cherry brandy on condition that he acknowledge the gift in the church magazine. The entry in the magazine read: "The Rector thanks Mr and Mrs So and So for the gift of fruit and the spirit in which it was given". I am grateful to the many people, both living and departed, for the friendship they gave and give me in so many places and for the generous spirit in which they gave and give.